MICHIGAN   BUSINESS   STUDIES
Volume II   Number 2
New Series

BANK FUNDS MANAGEMENT

Issues and Practices

Douglas A. Hayes

Division of Research
Graduate School of Business Administration
The University of Michigan

Library of Congress Cataloging in Publication Data
Hayes, Douglas Anderson, 1918–
  Bank funds management.

  (Michigan business studies; v. 2, no. 2)
  Includes bibliographical references.
  1. Bank investments.   2. Bank management.
I. Title.   II. Series.
HG1616.I5H39   332.1'7   80–10803
ISBN 0–87712–203–2
ISBN 0–87712–206–7 pbk.

CONTENTS

TABLES

FIGURES

PREFACE

The objectives of this book are twofold: (1) to discuss the major policy issues involved in the management of bank funds, exclusive of loan policies and programs which have been considered in a separate volume;[1] and (2) to set forth, compare, and evaluate the actual policies and implementation techniques of a selected sample of banks, stratified according to size and nature of their operations.

In essence, my concern is with those categories of assets and liabilities which for the most part are subject to regular discretionary control on the part of management. Although in theory it can be argued that all assets and liabilities are subject to such control, in practice this is not the case, except perhaps to a limited extent in the very long run. On the liability side, the provision of convenient and efficient services to customers in a competitive context generates a large proportion of the deposit universe. This means that a high degree of consistency in policies is highly desirable, if not absolutely necessary, and that modifications should be made only to obtain a competitive advantage in the relevant banking market or to protect the bank against competitive inroads by other institutions. In short, competitive and to some extent regulatory constraints strictly limit the policy options open to management.

On the asset side, and for generally the same reasons, a large proportion of the loan portfolio, especially with regard to amount and configuration, is not subject to management control. Banks must stand ready to meet the legitimate credit needs of their commercial (business) customers or be prepared to lose the relationships to competitors—an option, of course, which is generally unacceptable. In addition, if the services of a bank include major retail loan programs (largely installment, bankcard, and mortgage

1. Douglas A. Hayes, *Bank Lending Policies: Domestic and International,* 2d ed. (Ann Arbor: University of Michigan, Division of Research, Graduate School of Business Administration, 1977).

loans) involving extensive commitments to facilities, staff, and marketing efforts, customer demand rather than bank convenience will largely determine fund allocations to these markets, except perhaps during periods of severe strains in the financial markets when moderate curtailments may be possible. There is always the option, of course, of permanently abandoning some retail loan programs, but a management decision of this magnitude must be considered exceptional and nonrecurring.

Although a significant amount of the funds generated and allocated in banks is, as a practical matter, outside the operational control of funds management, at the same time a considerable amount is subject to such control. Indeed, in many banks the proportion has increased over the last decade or so. Over the years banks have typically enjoyed customer deposits in amounts which have exceeded loan program requirements, and this excess has been available for commitments to eligible financial assets on a purely impersonal basis. Up until the last twenty years or so, investment of such assets in the financial markets constituted the entire scope of discretionary funds management. As a consequence, it was conventional and reasonably accurate to categorize this phase of banking as an investment operation involving a mix of money market assets, government obligations, and municipal securities.

While management of investment portfolios still remains a significant activity, it is now in most banks merely a part of a larger framework of activities, and the broader term *funds management* has become more representative of the scope of responsibilities than the traditional term *investment management*. The innovation of liability instruments designed to purchase funds in the financial markets on an "as required" basis has been the primary factor responsible for this change. The result has been a significant increase in the number of policy options; indeed, certain aspects of funds management—interest arbitrage, for example—can be conducted almost independently of the customer-based banking process.

However, as the scope of funds management policies and the alternative vehicles for implementation have expanded, the range of appropriate policy differences between banks has also expanded, particularly as between banks in different size groups. The primary reason is that large banks have access to markets on both the asset and the liability sides that are not readily accessible to smaller banks. As a consequence, policies appropriate for large banks may be entirely inappropriate for banks of lesser size. In addition, the properties of the customer-based asset and liability universe tend to be different for banks of different sizes, and discretionary funds management policies should logically adjust to these differences. For example, fixed-rate consumer and mortgage loans often dominate the asset universes of community banks, which are usually of small or moderate size, whereas variable-rate commercial loans often dominate the asset structures of large banks. As a consequence, appropriate maturity policies for the asset sectors subject to discretionary control may be quite different. Therefore, in the several chapters dealing with topical phases of funds management policies, every effort has been made to consider separately policy formulation and implementation in banks of different size groups and operational characteristics.

It is hoped that the book might be useful to several clienteles. First, bank officers and committees responsible for funds management policies might obtain useful insights from the views of their peers on the various policy issues. In that connection, the choice of respondents was not based on random sampling; rather, respondents were carefully selected to include only banks with an outstanding reputation in this phase of bank management. Second, Schools of Banking whose objective is to improve the managerial capacities of bank officers usually include a course in funds management. These officers typically come from banks of widely different sizes, and one reason for the specific stratification of policies on the basis of size differences was to make the book more appropriate for such educational programs. Finally, my intention was to make the study useful as a reference work for courses in bank (financial institutions) management in Schools of Business Administration. The comparative views of high level bank officers on specific funds management policy issues may enrich and supplement academic courses in this area.

In structuring and writing this study, I have enjoyed the invaluable assistance of a number of individuals. In particular, Messrs. D. Dean Kaylor and Louis Betanzos of the National Bank of Detroit were most helpful in rendering assistance both in structuring the questionnaire and in selecting an appropriate list of respondents. I am most grateful for their counsel and cooperation. I would also like to express my deep appreciation to the officers of the respondent banks. In many instances they not only answered the specific questions as shown in the appendix, but also offered penetrating comments on a number of issues. In the relevant chapters I have quoted a number of these explanatory comments in order to suggest the subtle considerations which account for the variety of views on policy issues and implementation tactics. Finally, Dr. Alfred L. Edwards, Director of the Division of Research in the Graduate School of Business Administration, University of Michigan, gave strong support to the project, and in his division Ms. Helen Wilkinson typed much of the manuscript and Ms. Betsy Borda rendered invaluable assistance through careful editing of the material.

Douglas A. Hayes

Ann Arbor, Michigan
December, 1979

1

ECONOMIC CONTEXT
AND MANAGEMENT GOALS

The purposes of this chapter are: (1) to discuss briefly the economic context in which commercial banking services are provided, (2) to show the nature of the industry's structure, and (3) to analyze briefly the financial goals and constraints that are often employed as guidelines to management. Historically, for reasons indicated below, banks have been subject to more detailed and extensive governmental control than is typically the case in the private sector, although the pervasive extension of governmental regulations into all business activities makes this observation less accurate now than, say, twenty years ago. The nature of the more important regulatory constraints bearing on funds management will be considered briefly, along with those that banks might voluntarily impose in order to maintain the confidence of customers and the financial markets.

Nature of Banking Services

The banking industry offers a number of financial services to business firms, governmental units, and individuals. On the whole the major product lines are not differentiated, in the sense that patents, trademarks, and unique product design are unusual. Competition tends to be based partly on price, partly on convenience (location of service units), and perhaps most importantly on quality of service. The latter includes the timely rendering of consistent and accurate services in amounts and places and on terms that maximize customer satisfaction while at the same time producing reasonable profits for the bank.

The banking process may be described as a financial intermediation system in which the money balances and surplus funds of economic units are placed with banks on the condition that they will be available either on demand or after a prescribed time interval — usually less than a year but sometimes as much as four years or more. These funds are then used to

1

finance business, government, or consumer credit needs, either directly in the form of loans or indirectly in the form of security purchases in the secondary markets.

The financial services associated with this process are, first, the provision of interest-bearing instruments tailored to the needs and tastes of the fund providers. These instruments become the savings and time deposit liabilities of banks, but other funds may be acquired in the form of short-term borrowings that technically are differentiated from deposits but substantively are identical in terms of their legal liability properties. Second, funds placed with commercial banks as demand deposits subject to transfer via checks or electronic debit and credit systems represent the major transaction medium of exchange in the economic system. Price competition on these instruments is limited, since under existing law interest cannot be paid on such deposits per se. However, combination instruments which feature automatic transfers from interest-bearing savings deposits to demand deposits as needed to cover check payments are now offered by many banks.[1]

Commercial banks traditionally have emphasized the intermediation of these funds into customer loans, either in the form of individually structured commercial loans to established business firms or in the form of standardized installment loans, credit card charges, and real estate mortgages to individual consumers. But the asset structure also typically includes a substantial number of instruments acquired in the secondary financial markets. Government and municipal obligations of various maturities tend to dominate the investment portfolio, but money market instruments of various types may also be included. All must be creditor instruments, as equities are prohibited by law.

Funds management in the above context would include all policies designed to derive funds on the liability side (deposits and borrowings) and to allocate funds on the asset side (loans and investments). However, it is a fair assumption that consistent customer loan programs are necessary if a bank is to maintain its competitive position in the community. As a result, discretionary fund management policies for the most part accommodate to the requirements of established loan programs rather than the other way around.[2] Because our major purpose is a discussion of discretionary fund

1. In 1979, a court decision held that automatic transfer systems violated the statute prohibiting interest on demand deposits. As of late 1979, special legislation, which was expected to become law and thus to legalize these systems, was in process in Congress.

2. Like all broad assumptions, this one is open to some exceptions. In times of severe fund stringency, some restraints might be placed on certain sections of the loan portfolio. For a discussion of the limited options here, see Douglas A. Hayes, *Bank Lending Policies: Domestic and International,* 2d ed. (Ann Arbor: University of Michigan, Division of Research, Graduate School of Business Administration, 1977), pp. 228–34.

management policies and implementation tactics, the loan portfolio will be considered only to the extent that its configuration through time may operate as a constraint parameter on these policies.

Commercial banking: regulatory context

Banks are chartered and regulated under specific statutes of either the federal government (National Banking Act) or the several states. These statutes are highly detailed in nature and include many specific positive requirements and negative constraints.[3] Moreover, if a bank is a member of the Federal Reserve System (required for national banks and optional for state banks) or is insured under the Federal Deposit Insurance Act (a competitive necessity for practically all banks), then it is subject to additional statutory requirements and regulatory supervision. Historically, the major purpose of the unique governmental intrusion into the affairs of banks has been to "insure the safe and sound conduct of such business."[4] This regulatory objective is based on the historical fact that extensive failures of banks—particularly during the Great Depression of 1930–34—exacerbated considerably the extent and duration of cyclical declines.

While much of the regulatory structure remains oriented toward the "soundness" objective, in recent years a number of new regulatory objectives have emerged. These include (1) providing for consumer protection, (2) encouraging appropriate allocation of credit to community needs, (3) promoting adequate competition in the industry, and (4) encouraging the allocation of bank credit to certain areas defined as desirable for public policy reasons.[5]

Because the banking statutes include numerous regulatory specifics, it is difficult to cite all those that might be relevant to fund management policies. However, the following would be of major significance:

Liability constraints:

1. Interest payments on demand deposits are prohibited by statute and payments on time and savings deposits are subject to regulatory limits. The Federal Reserve imposes the limits (known as Regulation Q), and they are applicable to all FDIC-insured banks. The limits can and have changed from time to time; the current specifics will be

---

3. For example, in Michigan the statute runs to eight chapters consisting of forty-three pages of fine print and is formally cited as the "Banking Code of 1969." *Act No. 319, Public Acts of 1969.*

4. Ibid., Chapter 1, sec. 2.

5. The possible conflicts between these more recent regulatory objectives and the historically dominant "soundness" objective should be evident. If intensive competition is strongly encouraged, for example, then some banks would obviously become more subject to failure because of inability to respond to competitive pressures.

shown in the appropriate chapter. Recent changes have been in the direction of relaxing Reg Q constraints to a considerable degree, and complete elimination must be regarded as an ultimate possibility.

2. Short-term nondeposit borrowings are not specifically limited as to amounts or rates, but the extent of exposure may be subject to regulatory evaluation.

3. Minimum capital requirements are imposed on new banks and the "adequacy" of capital is evaluated on an ongoing basis. The issue of capital adequacy has long been a major point of tension and controversy between banks and the regulatory authorities, as bank management correctly perceives that excessively high capital standards make it difficult to earn an adequate return on such capital. Specific and unambiguous quantitative guidelines are difficult to determine, but it appears that capital consisting of 6 to 8 percent of assets and 9 to 12 percent of risk assets (defined as all assets except cash and U.S. government or agency obligations) represents rough regulatory targets, although ad hoc negotiations on the subject of capital adequacy seem to be the rule rather than the exception.

Asset constraints:

1. Banks are required to hold legal reserves (cash or equivalent for Federal Reserve member banks) as a percentage of deposits, with percentages generally lower against time and savings deposits than against demand deposits.[6]

2. Earning assets are confined to debt obligations (securities or loans) of government units, corporations, or individuals. With a few trivial exceptions, no equity-type assets can be acquired.

3. U.S. government, government agency, or general obligations of states or municipal units can be acquired in any amount.

4. All other securities or loans, except those guaranteed by the government, are limited as to the amounts that can be made to a single borrower. The limit is expressed as a percentage of the capital accounts. This is known as the "legal limit" and is equal to 10 percent of specified capital accounts in the case of national banks; state laws are often somewhat more liberal.[7]

5. Marketable obligations are valued at amortized cost on the financial

---

6. The original purpose of legal reserve requirements was to promote the soundess objective. However, it is now conceded that the major purpose is to enable the Federal Reserve to carry out discretionary monetary policy through control of the legal reserve base and consequently of total deposits of the banking system.

7. Overnight loans to other banks in the Federal Funds market are usually excluded from legal limit restrictions.

statements if they are of adequate credit quality. Other bonds, unless specific exceptions are made, must be carried at market value.[8]

6. For banks that operate as dealers in government securities, dealer-originated positions must be held in a separate trading account carried on the books at the lower of cost or market.

7. Loans and nonrated investments are subject to regulatory evaluation, and writedowns or writeoffs of doubtful credits can be required. Indeed, the quality of the entire earning asset portfolio is subject to regulatory evaluation and comment.

Industry Structure

Under existing law, banks are chartered for a specific home office location and may then establish branches as permitted by statute. State law varies widely in this respect; some states allow statewide branching (California) and some prohibit all branches (Illinois). The National Banking Act specifies that national banks in a given state must conform to the branching provisions of state law, and interstate branching is prohibited unless reciprocity is specifically authorized in the statutes of particular states. At the present time, no state allows banks chartered in another state to operate branches therein.

The development of bank holding companies as authorized under special legislation in the early seventies has extended the geographic limits of effective banking operations in states where such multibank holding companies are permitted. Holding company systems have expanded rapidly in recent years, but in many cases banks within the system retain considerable autonomy of management. Indeed, for regulatory examination and evaluation purposes each bank in a holding system is considered completely independent and is treated accordingly.

Although the full effects of the holding company trend have yet to be determined, the structure of the banking industry would seem divisible into three major categories: (1) the money center banks, (2) the major regional banks, and (3) the local community banks. The money center banks are a few very large banks which obtain and allocate funds on a worldwide basis. To a considerable extent, their operations represent purchases and sales of funds of large unit size in the impersonal financial markets of the world. The major regionals have much of their business concentrated in a large city and its environs, but in most instances they also engage to a moderate degree in national and international activities. The local community banks

8. In annual reports of bank holding companies subject to SEC reporting requirements, a footnote to the position statement is required to show the market value of the entire portfolio.

are those that obtain and allocate funds largely within a given city, town, or suburban area. Most emphasize retail banking (deposits of and loans to individuals), but they also offer services to all types of businesses within their communities.

The available published data do not classify banks along these functional lines, but reasonable inferences as to the relative numbers and size of each category might be derived from the data in Table 1-1. The money center

TABLE 1-1

Number and Size Distribution of Commercial Banks
(As of December 31, 1976)

	Range of Assets (in Millions of Dollars)					
	0–100	100–500	500–1,000	1,000–5,000	over 5,000	Total
Number	13,546	902	120	112	18	14,698
Percentage of Total	92.1	6.1	0.9	0.8	0.1	100.0
Total Assets of Group (in Billions)	$291.3	$180.9	$85.4	$213.8	$264.6	$1,036.0
Percentage of Total	28.1	17.5	8.4	20.5	25.5	100.0

Source: Federal Deposit Insurance Corporation, *Annual Report for 1976*, p. 242.

banks are all included in the category of banks with assets of $5 billion or more. These banks represent only 0.1 percent of the universe but control 25 percent of total bank assets. Of the 18 banks with assets in excess of $5 billion, only 11 — the largest institutions in New York and Chicago, plus the Bank of America in California — are generally regarded as money center institutions. The other 7, plus the 112 with assets between $1 billion and $5 billion, comprise the major regionals. They represent slightly less than 1 percent of the total number but control about 25 percent of total bank assets. Finally, banks in the local community category represent 99 percent of the total number and control somewhat in excess of 50 percent of total assets.

It is clear that the banking structure is highly heterogeneous in nature, ranging from small banks wherein fund management policies are necessarily very restricted in scope to a few money center institutions with unique worldwide fund management operations. This study will eliminate both extremes and concentrate on the fund management policies of the major regionals (those banks with more than $1 billion in assets) and the local community banks. The latter are divided into two subsets, those with assets between $50 million and $300 million and those with assets between

$300 million and $1 billion. The total universe includes about 75 percent of total banking assets and probably about 50 percent of the total number of banks. The reasons for excluding the extremes are diametrically opposite: in the one case policy options are too limited to allow for a useful study, and in the other they are so extensive that the policies of a very few unique institutions would dominate the entire study.

Financial dynamics

Because banks are constrained to lend and invest only in debt obligations, must pay interest costs on a large portion of the funds so used, and also must meet other operating expenses such as salaries and occupancy costs, the net earnings margins on assets are necessarily moderate.[9] Substantial leverage is therefore required in order to obtain a reasonable return on capital. The relationships between these several factors are illustrated in Table 1-2. The data do not represent a precise formulation of the funds intermediation relationships because both operating income and expenses include minor amounts derived or incurred from ancillary activities such as trust services. However, the data should represent a reasonable approximation of the financial dynamics that characterize the banking process.

It can be observed that the return on capital varies directly with the amount of the net interest margin and the ratio of assets to capital accounts and inversely with the amount of interest costs and operating expenses incurred per dollar of assets employed. In addition, moderate use of borrowed capital funds, in essence "double leverage," may increase the return on equity capital above that obtained on total capital.

But policies aimed at maximization of net interest margins and capital leverage also presumably have risk dimensions. Although the relationships might not be exact, relative asset yields on loans and investments tend to be correlated with various degrees of risk, and greater leverage of course means that the capital protection afforded depositor funds is diminished. Therefore, trade-offs are necessarily required and fund management policies must be designed in such a way as to balance returns available on alternative asset decisions with a tolerable risk exposure related to capital levels.

If it is assumed that risk or regulatory considerations will ultimately have the effect of constraining policies designed to improve the net interest margin and to increase leverage, then the long-term growth in both earnings per share and in total asset size exclusive of acquisitions should depend

9. Interest costs as a percentage of assets will vary with the deposit mix (demand deposits have zero interest costs but higher operating service costs) and the types and maturities of the savings and time instruments. Demand deposits tend to be relatively higher as a percentage of total deposits in larger banks, but such banks often use a greater proportion of Regulation Q-exempt funds on which interest costs are usually higher than on Reg Q-limited deposits.

TABLE 1-2

Operating Ratios of Member Banks
(Seventh Federal Reserve District; as of 1977)

	Asset Size (in Millions of Dollars)		
	50–100	100–300	Over 300
Percentage of Assets:			
Operating income	7.46%	7.23%	7.38%
Interest costs	3.70	3.58	3.53
Net interest margin*	3.76%	3.65%	3.85%
Other operating expenses and taxes	2.85	2.76	3.05
Net income	.91%	.89%	.80%
Assets to Capital Accounts	13.4	13.3	13.4
Return on Total Capital:			
$\frac{\text{Net income}}{\text{Assets}} \times \frac{\text{Assets}}{\text{Capital}}$	12.2%	11.8%	10.7%
Return on Equity Capital	12.9%	12.8%	11.5%

Source: Federal Reserve Board of Chicago.

*Technically, *net interest margin* is usually defined as the net percentage return on earning assets rather than total assets; in subsequent chapters this definition will be used. Unfortunately, published macro data on the banking industry do not show the net interest margin based on earning assets alone, so returns on total assets have been used as a proxy.

largely on the internal growth rate in equity capital. The specific assumptions are: (1) growth in deposits and also perhaps borrowed funds can be obtained at reasonable costs but will be limited to the capital growth rate; (2) the capital structure already incorporates an optimal amount of long-term subordinated debt; (3) economies of scale of operating expenses will be asymtotic (in other words, it becomes increasingly difficult to lower their amount as a percentage of total assets); and (4) the external sale of new shares will be infrequent.

Given these assumptions, the growth rate in earnings can be expressed by the following simple model:

Rg = Re(1-P0), where
Rg = growth rate in earnings,
Re = return on equity, and
P0 = percentage of earnings paid out in dividends.

It should be apparent that this expression represents the internal growth rate in book value per share or, as some analysts prefer, the earnings retention rate expressed as a percentage of book value. One final caveat might be made: for the expression to hold, deposits and other fund sources must show a growth rate equal to the earnings retention rate, and in some circumstances this may be difficult to achieve in a prudent manner. Therefore, one cannot automatically assume that increasing the internal growth rate by lowering the payout ratio will necessarily result in a commensurate growth in earnings.

Determination of long-term goals

On the basis of the above discussion it is possible to suggest a methodology for the determination of specific long-term goals and constraints. The logical starting point would be two major objectives accompanied by one constraint. These would be (1) return on assets,[10] (2) return on equity (capital), and (3) ratio of equity (capital) to total assets. The assumption is that the major objective is to maximize the long-term rate of return to shareholders within the limits imposed by risk and regulatory constraints.

The next step is for the bank (holding company) to establish its long-term growth goals.[11] The growth potential for the relevant banking market and a reasonable appraisal of the bank's prospective market share are, of course, the fundamental controlling parameters, and for that reason the specific goals may legitimately vary widely. On the basis of ongoing market analysis and past experience, projected growth rates for customer deposits can be targeted. In larger banks, the ability to increase usage of borrowed funds from noncustomer sources might also be included. Given the estimated liability growth rates, capital needs can be estimated. If the expected return on equity combined with a reasonable earnings retention rate can provide the required capital growth, then further goals need not be specified; otherwise, estimates of future external debt or equity issues can be incorporated into the set of long-term objectives, and their impact on earnings per share evaluated.

10. A slight modification would be to break down the return on assets into its components: (1) net interest margin and (2) ratio of operating expenses to assets.

11. A research study on the properties that differentiate price-earnings ratios of bank stocks found that differences in the rate and stability of earnings growth, along with location in geographic areas perceived as having above-average growth, were the principal factors accounting for P/E differences. It may be noted, however, that the study was based on evidence prior to the recession of 1974–75, when media visibility given to problems of the banking industry may have changed the importance of the growth rate in determining relative P/E ratios. R. A. Schick and V. A. Verbrugge, "An Analysis of Bank Price-Earnings Ratios," *Journal of Bank Research,* Summer 1975, pp. 148–49.

Once these steps are accomplished, the long-term potential growth rate in earnings per share can be computed. This figure, of course, is of major concern to the stockholder constituency. As a parenthetical note, it can be argued that instead of assigning a specific number to each target, management could substitute a reasonable range to indicate clearly that the several goals are derived from an estimation process involving uncertain future events.

On the asset side, long-term objectives would logically begin with an appraisal of the outlook for the established loan programs, followed by the setting of goals for these programs consistent with fund availability and capital support. The methodology traditionally established for determining this relationship has been to set a maximum or optimal range for the loan-deposit ratio. Alternatively, a target for risk assets (all assets except cash and governments) as a percentage of capital may be substituted for the loan-deposit ratio. Planning objectives for other earning asset categories are not required because they are residual in nature: the investment portfolio (including money market assets) will receive any funds not required for loan programs. In the past some banks have set a liquidity constraint in the form of a prescribed ratio of liquid assets to deposits, but as liquidity requirements are now often met from liability management (purchased funds), this constraint has generally been dropped.

Financial Goals and Constraints: Empirical Evidence

Table 1–3 shows the replies of respondent banks with respect to various specific goal options. The note to Table 1–3 indicates the frequency of mention of other goals. It is notable that all respondents had several specific financial goals and all but two had established specific constraints as well. Unanimity was evidenced on only one goal, return on assets, but only a few banks failed to specify return on equity (capital), earnings growth, and the dividend-payout ratio. Opinion was divided, however, as to the need for specific growth objectives in deposits and assets. The majority set targets for deposits and asset growth, but a significant minority apparently regarded them as unnecessary.

In the purchased funds area, the responses show that a large proportion of banks with assets of less than $1 billion considered it inappropriate to target their growth. Two reasons might be suggested for this view: (1) many banks use short-time borrowings only infrequently to meet temporary liquidity needs; and (2) large certificates of deposit in these banks are offered to customers only on an accommodation basis and are not actively solicited. The large banks were divided almost equally on the need for growth limits on purchased funds; in their case, as the total amount might

TABLE 1-3

Frequencies of Specific Financial Goals and Constraints
(Respondent Banks; as of 1978)

	Asset Size (in Millions of Dollars)					
	To 300		300–1,000		Over 1,000	
	Yes	No	Yes	No	Yes	No
Earnings Goals:						
Return on assets	12	0	12	0	9	0
Return on equity (capital)	10	2	11	1	8	1
Growth Goals:						
Earnings growth	11	1	11	1	9	0
Deposit growth:						
Core	6	6	9	3	6	3
Purchased funds	2	10	3	12	4	5
Total asset growth	8	4	9	3	5	4
Dividend payout ratio	11	1	10	2	6	3
Constraints:	12	0	10	2	9	0
Total capital to assets	10	2	9	1	8	1
Equity capital to assets	7	5	8	2	8	1
Capital to deposits	9	3	6	3	5	3
Loan-deposit ratio	12	0	10	0	8	1
Capital to risk assets	8	4	4	6	6	3
Governments to deposits	1	11	2	8	2	7

Note: Other goals and constraints mentioned: share of market (2), net interest margins (5), productivity (assets per employee) (2).

be related to dealer operations and interest arbitrage opportunities, specific targets might be regarded as inappropriate.[12] However, given the greater cost and reliability risks associated with purchased funds, as opposed to core deposits, a strong argument can be made that is is desirable to set limits on their use in some way.

The constraints sector of Table 1–3 shows that most respondent banks had specified one or more capital adequacy ratios; probably because the ratios of total capital and equity capital to total assets are typically used in the regulatory appraisal of capital adequacy, most banks expressed their formal constraint in these terms. Because the risk asset-to-capital ratio is

12. The various options involved in the use of purchased funds will be discussed in more detail in the chapters on liquidity and spread management.

widely used in regulatory appraisals, it was somewhat surprising that a number of banks did not indicate a specific constraint here.[13]

However, the traditional loan-to-deposit ratio may be considered a proxy constraint on risk assets, as loans represent by far the major risk asset category. With one exception, all respondents had established an optimal and/or maximum level for this ratio. In a theoretical sense, this ratio is deficient because risk assets may include significant amounts held in the investment portfolio as distinguished from the loan portfolio, but bank stock analysts often use this ratio in comparative appraisals of banks. Too low a ratio is considered a manifestation of a lack of aggressiveness and too high a ratio a sign of strain, where low and high are based on peer group averages.

Because government obligations represent the main source of liquidity on the asset side, and because by regulatory definition they represent the major riskless earning asset, it can be argued that an appropriate ratio of governments to deposits might be established. However, only five respondents considered a target here to be desirable. The evidence suggests that the government portfolio is no longer regarded as sacrosanct and, therefore, its amount may vary widely through time. There are still perhaps minimum needs for government obligations based on "window dressing" perceptions and perhaps pledging needs against public deposits, but governments otherwise are apparently regarded as merely one of the available options in the universe of eligible financial assets.

Financial ratios: empirical data

In establishing financial goals and constraints, each bank (or holding company) presumably uses its prior experience as the starting point and then makes such adjustments as appear reasonable on the basis of evaluation of future long-term prospects. As the economic properties of geographic areas vary widely, considerable differences in target goals can be expected among various banks. However, as a rough indication of possible targets for the major financial goals cited in Table 1–3, the data in Table 1–4 covering member banks of the seventh Federal Reserve district may be useful. These data suggest that large banks tend to have somewhat lower returns on assets but greater capital leverage than smaller banks. However,

---

13. In May of 1978 the federal regulatory agencies (FDIC, Federal Reserve, and Comptroller of Currency) announced the adoption of a new uniform system for evaluating the condition of banks subject to their jurisdiction. The major quantitative appraisal of capital adequacy in the system was given as the ratio of risk assets (defined as all assets except cash and due from banks, government and agency securities, Fed Funds sold, and securities purchased under agreement to resell) to total capital plus valuation reserves. Given this dominant stature of the risk asset-to-capital ratio, more banks may well include it in their list of specified constraints. *Examination Report CAMEL Rating Form*, p. 2, as attached to FDIC News Release 52–78.

TABLE 1-4

Financial Ratio Ranges
(Seventh District Member Banks; 1974-77)

	Asset Size (in Millions of Dollars)		
	50–100	100–300	Over 300†
Return on assets (%)	0.81– 0.94	0.81– 0.91	0.69– 0.82
Return on equity (%)	11.1 –13.4	11.0 –13.1	10.0 –11.8
Dividend payout ratio (%)	29.9 –32.5	31.3 –42.7	38.5 –47.5
Capital accounts to assets (%)	7.7 – 8.4	7.5 – 8.1	6.1 – 7.7
Capital risk assets (%)	10.2 –10.8	10.3 –11.1	8.7 – 9.9
Loans to deposits*	60.2	58.6	70.5

Source: Federal Reserve Bank of Chicago, *Seventh District Member Banks, Operating Ratios.*

*Published only in 1977.

†Average of banks with foreign offices and those without such offices.

the large bank data may be distorted by inclusion of a relatively few very large banks with extensive interest arbitrage operations and dealer positions in Fed Funds and Eurodollars on both sides of their position statement. These positions, which essentially are offsets, should be eliminated to make their statements comparable to those of other banks. Assuming such an adjustment, the range of target goals for well-managed banks might be estimated as follows:

Return on assets	0.8–1.0%
Return on equity	12– 15%
Dividend payout ratios	30– 50%
Capital accounts to assets	7– 8%
Capital to risk assets	10– 12%
Loans to deposits	60– 75%

The internal long-term growth rates consistent with those goals would range between about 6 and 11 percent.[14] While these growth rates are moderately higher than those obtained in the corporate sector as a whole, it seems reasonable that a well-managed institution should not accept the average corporate growth rate as a long-term objective but should strive to show a performance in excess of the average.

14. This is based on the internal growth rate model: $Rg = Re(1-PO)$. A return on equity of 12 percent with a payment of 50 percent results in a 6 percent growth rate, while a return on equity of 15 percent with a payment of 30 percent results in a growth rate of 10.5 percent.

2

THE BANKING PROCESS:
NATURE AND TRENDS

During the past two decades the banking process has shown the most radical changes since the latter part of the nineteenth century, when demand deposits replaced bank notes (currency) as the principal source of bank funds. As these deposits are our principal transaction medium of exchange, commercial banks have traditionally been distinguished from other financial intermediaries largely on the basis of their unique role in the monetary system.

Prior to the decade of the sixties, when demand deposits dominated the liability structure, the following set of fund usage priorities was conventionally considered appropriate for commercial banks:

1. An adequate amount of primary reserves in the form of cash and deposits with other banks, including legal reserve deposits at the Federal Reserve banks, should have first priority in the fund allocation process. But policies should be aimed at minimizing primary reserves because they provided no returns to the bank.

2. Secondary reserves in the form of short-term, high-quality marketable securities should have second priority in order to meet both anticipated and unexpected fluctuations in demand deposits. This was considered necessary to provide adequate protective liquidity, and to enable the bank to minimize its primary reserve position.

3. Customer loans, defined as credit accommodation to corporate and individual demand depositors, should have third priority, as reasonably liberal loan policies were considered necessary to compete effectively for demand deposits.

4. Open market bond investments should represent the residual use of deposits not needed to satisfy the above priorities; some of these investments should be held in short-term maturities to meet possible loan demands of both existing and prospective customers for whom

14

loan accommodation is the major quid pro quo for their deposit accounts.[1]

Although savings and time deposits were also accepted, they were considered to be a peripheral source of funds primarily required to meet demands for real estate loans, which then as now were legally limited to a specified fraction of such deposits.[2]

The new liability structure

The data in Table 2-1 show that the heavy emphasis on the policy issues related to demand deposit intermediation appeared reasonable as recently as perhaps 1962. Since then, however, the nature of the liability structure (source of bank funds) has undergone a radical transformation. Whereas demand deposits in 1960 represented 64 percent of fund sources (exclusive of capital), by 1970 the figure was less than 40 percent. Moreover, their relative importance has continued to erode so that by 1978 demand deposits represented only 26 percent of the noncapital funds of member banks. In brief, while for more than half a century banks were largely regarded as demand deposit institutions with a peripheral concern for savings and time deposits, the data in Table 2-1 clearly show that the opposite is now the case. In addition, nondeposit borrowings have emerged as a significant source of funds.

Interest sensitivity

A second major change in the nature of bank liabilities, which the aggregative data in Table 2-1 do not effectively capture, is that an increasing proportion of the total liabilities have become "interest-sensitive," in that they are acquired at market interest rates and are relatively short-term in nature. Most mature and must be rolled over at prevailing interest rates within thirty days to six months. The liabilities currently included in this category are short-term borrowings, certificates of deposit with denominations of $100,000 or more, and the six-month money market certificates ($10,000 minimum denomination) on which rates are pegged to Treasury bill rates of similar maturity. Until 1970, because all time deposits were subject to Regulation Q limits, only short-term borrowings were interest-sensitive in nature; moreover, such borrowings were of minor amounts except during periods of severe disintermediation such as 1969–70.[3]

---

1. R. I. Robinson, *The Management of Bank Funds* (New York: McGraw-Hill, 1962), pp. 13–18.

2. Ibid., p. 286.

3. Regulation Q rate limits on CDs of $100,000 and above were first suspended in June of

TABLE 2-1

Selected Asset and Liability Data
(Member Banks: 1960–78)

Year	Assets			
	Securities		Loans*	Fed Funds Sold†
	Governments	Municipals		
1960	49.1	14.1	99.9	—
1962	53.0	20.8	118.6	—
1964	48.7	28.4	147.7	—
1966	41.9	33.8	181.6	2.1
1968	47.9	48.4	215.7	5.6
1970	45.4	55.7	241.8	12.7
1972	48.7	69.6	310.0	20.0
1974	55.9	70.9	400.0	29.8
3/31/77	92.7	74.8	405.6	35.2
3/31/78	92.9	80.8	460.0	35.1

Year	Liabilities			
	Deposits‡		Short-Term Borrowings	Capital
	Adjusted Demand	Savings & Time		
1960	94.6	53.5	.1	16.8
1962	101.5	79.7	3.6	19.9
1964	108.3	103.6	2.5	22.9
1966	112.9	129.8	4.6	26.3
1968	131.5	163.5	8.5	30.1
1970	133.2	179.8	18.6	34.1
1972	158.4	240.2	36.4	41.2
1974	165.9	305.9	52.8	48.2
3/31/77	165.8	351.6	70.5	59.5
3/31/78	167.5	387.9	84.6	64.8

Source: Federal Reserve bulletins.

*Gross loans used to make figures comparable for entire period.

†Includes securities purchased under resale agreements in 1974 and subsequent years.

‡Excludes interbank deposits in both demand and time categories and float in case of demand deposits.

1970 for maturities of between 30 and 59 days and in May of 1973 for all other maturities. Until those dates Regulation Q limits on rates constrained their interest-sensitivity, but also made them subject to disintermediation at times when open market rates on competitive instruments exceeded the Reg Q limits. Money market certificates pegged to the Treasury bill rate were first authorized on June 1, 1978, and have since increased to significant amounts in most banks.

Table 2–2 indicates the major shift in the composition of time and savings deposits toward the large CDs that has been experienced by the large weekly reporting banks. In addition, short-term borrowings, also interest-sensitive in nature, have increased at a rapid rate. The net result has been a remarkable increase in the relative amounts of interest-sensitive liabilities of large banks: in 1979 they represented about 64 percent of the liabilities subject to explicit interest costs as compared to about 35 percent in mid-1970 and only 6.5 percent at the end of 1965.

Unfortunately, since similar data for banks other than the large weekly reporting banks have not been available until recently, long-term trends for moderate-sized banks cannot be specifically indicated.[4] However, the liability composition of these banks as of September 30, 1978, is shown in Table 2–3. These data suggest that, although the proportion of interest-sensitive items in the liability composition of smaller banks has increased, the percentage was of far different proportions than was the case for large banks. It is well known, however, that even in moderate-sized banks money market certificates increased rapidly during 1979. Because of this

TABLE 2–2

Composition of Liabilities Subject to Interest Costs
(Weekly Reporting Commercial Banks; in Billions of Dollars)

| | Regulation Q-Controlled | | Regulation Q-Exempt* | | |
Date	Savings	Time†	Large CDs	Borrowings‡	% Exempt
12/28/65	47.1	42.3	—	6.2	6.5
7/1/70	46.4	41.1	14.1	32.2	34.6
4/31/72	57.6	56.0	35.5	31.5	37.1
5/29/74	57.8	62.3	79.5	63.4	54.3
5/25/76	80.1	46.8	96.1	58.3	54.5
5/31/78	93.4	52.0	119.8	94.3	59.8
5/31/79	76.6	54.3	118.0	109.5	63.5

Source: Federal Reserve bulletins.

*It is assumed here that virtually all large CDs were exempt from Reg Q after removal of limits, although some continued to be controlled until 1973.

†Includes nonnegotiable large CDs until 1976 because these were not reported separately until then. As a consequence, data prior to 1976 overstate amount of Reg Q-limited deposits. Also, money market certificates included in this category as of 5/31/79 are not reported separately.

‡Includes Fed Funds purchased, borrowings from Federal Reserve and others, and obligations of home office to foreign branches. The latter represents Eurodollar borrowings.

4. The Federal Reserve first published the breakdown of the composition of liabilities for all commercial banks as of March 31, 1977.

TABLE 2-3

Composition of Liabilities Subject to Interest Costs
(Moderate-Sized Banks; in Billions of Dollars)

| | Regulation Q-Controlled | | | Regulation Q-Exempt | | | | | |
Date	Savings	Time	Total	Large CDs	Borrowings	Total	Grand Total	% Exempt
9/30/78	155.3	143.5	298.8	72.5	21.2	93.7	392.5	23.9

Source: Federal Reserve bulletin, July 1979, p. A19.

fact and the probable further relaxation of Reg Q, it seems probable that
interest-sensitive liabilities will soon represent a large proportion of the
total in most banks. Particularly during periods of high interest rates (such
as 1979), the transfer from the Reg Q-limited universe to the interest-
sensitive universe can be expected to proceed at a fairly rapid rate. This
massive shift in the properties of bank liabilities in recent years has
necessarily resulted in a new "ball game" for funds management, and the
policy issues related thereto will be heavily emphasized in subsequent
chapters.

Fund Intermediation: Core Funds

Core funds are those obtained from customers who regularly use one or
more banking services on an ongoing personal basis. They include the following categories: (1) all demand deposits, (2) Reg Q-limited savings and
time accounts, and (3) money market certificates and large CDs purchased
from customers from whom the bank will receive consistent preference in
placement if rates are reasonably close to market levels. In addition,
amounts obtained from Fed Funds purchased and securities repurchase
agreements (repos) might be construed as core funds to the extent that they
result from services offered to correspondent banks or corporate customers.
The definition suggests the major criterion for distinguishing purchased
funds from core funds: the former consist of funds acquired on a purely
impersonal, competitive-bid basis in the money markets, whereas the latter
are based on some type of customer relationship. In the case of a few relatively large money center banks (principally in New York), the source of
core funds may extend over a wide area and may even include a significant
number of foreign customers. But for most banks, by far the major proportion of core funds is obtained from business firms, local government units,
and households within a geographic area reasonably close to the head office
and branches of the bank.

In a general sense, core funds, after provision for appropriate liquidity,
have traditionally been the means of funding commercial and retail loan

programs. Commercial loans represent credit extended to the business and local government sectors of the community. It is here that the feedback effect between sources and usage of funds has traditionally been evident; in return for deposit accounts, financial services are rendered, of which the most important is the extension of loans individually structured to the needs of the borrower. Indeed, this feedback relationship is formally introduced into loan pricing policies, in that a major determinant of rates on commercial loans is the amount of the supporting deposit balances that customers hold on average with the bank.

In retail loan programs the linkage between deposits and loans is largely absent. Individuals and, perhaps, very small business units hold the deposits for money transaction purposes (demand) or for savings purposes (savings and time accounts of moderate amounts). The ability to offer convenient and attractive packages of deposit instruments is of great importance in attracting these deposits; rates paid on savings and time accounts may also be important, depending on the alternatives available locally and on the size distribution of the accounts.

On the asset side, installment loans, mortgages, and credit card usage represent the major retail loan programs, although small business loans may also be included in this category. The terms of these credits are for the most part standardized, and they are offered on a mass basis to persons of reasonable credit standing. Volume is important because economies of scale tend to be significant.

Fund management: core funds

Given a set of continuing commercial relationships and established retail loan programs, management of core funds on a discretionary basis usually has two dimensions. First, there is a liquidity dimension arising from the fact that their supply or their interest-sensitivity properties may not move in harmony with the demand for and interest-sensitivity properties of commercial and retail loans. As a consequence, liquidity management involves effective control of the interest-sensitivity position as well as the maintenance of adequate sources of funds to meet situations where the demand for loans is increasing more rapidly than the supply of core funds. Planning policy options for liquidity needs and making tactical decisions as to which options are optimal for meeting these needs are significant managerial functions in core funds intermediation and will be discussed in some detail in Chapter 3.

The second dimension of discretionary management of core funds results from the fact that over extended time periods these funds generally provide amounts in excess of those required for loans and even for asset liquidity needs. Therefore, most banks have discretionary investment portfolios, the objective of which is to maximize returns without exceeding a tolerable degree of risk exposure. Government obligations, besides representing a source of liquid assets, may be of some importance here, but typically it is municipal obligations which have come to dominate the investment account. Therefore, alternative policies and tactics for managing both government and municipal portfolios will be considered in some detail in subsequent chapters.

Fund Intermediation: Spread Banking

In a narrow sense spread banking can be defined as the acquisition of funds through competitive bidding on a rate basis and their concurrent intermediation into impersonally acquired financial assets. Presumably the yields of these assets will exceed fund costs, resulting in a positive yield spread. *Interest arbitrage* is the term generally used to describe this operation. Arbitrage in a pure sense is the simultaneous purchase and sale at zero risk of essentially the same instrument in different markets, wherein market imperfections lead to a spread opportunity. In a spread banking operation, the liability purchased and the asset acquired may have different properties (often a maturity difference); as a consequence, spread management only partially concurs with the strict definition of arbitrage. This caveat is important because spread banking usually involves the conscious assumption of a certain amount of risk in the expectation of generating returns.

Because a large proportion of large CDs and short-term borrowings presumably are obtained on a competitive rate basis and breakouts of these categories are available in the banking data, it is tempting to conclude that the spread banking sector can be measured by its totals in the banking system. In the absence of more refined classifications of the data, these amounts might be used as a very rough proxy for this sector; however, there are several factors associated with the policies governing the acquisition and usage of these funds which complicate the picture.

First, as discussed above, indeterminate amounts of large CDs and borrowings are obtained from core deposit and loan customers, for whom yield spread opportunities may not control the decision to acquire the funds. Because of the customer relationship, corporate and governmental customers may place funds with their local banks at a rate less than the maximum obtainable in the market; sometimes a sacrifice of as much as 50 basis points will be regarded as tolerable. Moreover, banks usually feel some obligation to purchase the short-term money of such customers at reasonably competitive rates even though attractive spread opportunities at tolerable risk levels are not available. In short, purchasing the temporary excess funds of regular customers at reasonably competitive rates has become a part of the service mix rendered to such customers. [5]

---

5. The following statement, taken from an annual report, is illustrative: "While we accommodate our customer requirements for large certificate of deposit placements, it is our

Second, in large banks an indeterminate part of short-term borrowings, particularly Federal Funds, represents takings resulting from a dealer operation rather than a spread banking operation. As dealers, banks must constantly furnish bid-ask quotations on the instrument—Fed Funds, for example—and the net amount bought or sold will be a function of customer requirements rather than dealer bank needs. In order for the bank to remain visible in the market as an active dealer, rates on both the bid and ask sides must be reasonably in line with the national market at all times; if not, market participants, such as correspondents, that ordinarily contact the large bank to buy or sell Fed Funds not only may drop the bank from their contact list but may also remove part or all of their other business.[6] In a sense, the spread realized from the difference between the bid-ask quotations, even though possibly only a few basis points, allows the activity to be construed as a form of spread banking, but essentially it is a dealer trading operation rather than a spread banking operation.

Finally, some purchased funds in the form of CDs and borrowings may result from liquidity management of the core customer activities and, therefore, do not represent funds acquired to implement a spread banking operation. Outside of accommodating customers' needs as noted above, it is probable that for most banks outside the money centers liquidity requirements rather than deliberate spread opportunities are the major determinant of purchased fund usage. In this case the amounts of purchased funds will increase or decrease in response to variations in the loan and core fund sectors of the bank. To a large extent, therefore, the usage of purchased funds may be a consequence of liquidity management rather than a discretionary interest arbitrage operation.

Because of these complications the quantitative dimensions of spread banking operations are difficult to measure. But because large CDs and short-term borrowings in large banks have shown a long-term growth well in excess of loan funding requirements, it is probable that spread banking has become an increasingly significant activity in these banks, and even some smaller banks may engage in these operations to some extent.

In core fund intermediation, competition for customers from other banks

---

policy not to purchase these funds in any significant amounts from outside sources in order to fund loan demand and investment acquisitions." Security Bancorp, Inc., *Annual Report for 1977* (Southgate, Mich.: 1978), p. 3. This policy statement suggests that spread banking in this case is essentially an involuntary adjunct to the package of services offered to core deposit customers.

6. For example, a small bank might hold a demand deposit account with a large bank in its vicinity in return for check collection and other services. Ability to sell or buy legal reserves (Fed Funds) on a given day at competitive rates would be among the expected services. If this service was not rendered on a regular basis, the small bank might decide to change its correspondent relationship.

and nonbank financial institutions requires relative conformity in policy matters, thus constraining major departures from competitive norms; in pure spread banking operations, however, each institution can exercise wide discretion in determining appropriate policies because competitive feedbacks are minimal. Consequently, it might be expected that wide variations in spread banking policies will prevail within the universe of banks at a given time and even at different times within the same bank. Indeed, a significant number of banks have a definitive policy of avoiding discretionary spread banking as defined above. The discussion of policies with respect to this phase of modern banking will therefore be applicable only to a subset of the universe of respondent banks rather than to the entire group.

Bank Fund Intermediation: Composite

Table 2-4 shows the composition of assets and liabilities of commercial banks in the U.S. divided into two groups: (1) large banks which have assets of at least $750 million; and (2) all other banks, including some of significant size and many more of small size, with assets totaling a few million dollars. While more stratified data would be preferable to indicate the asset and liability structure of banks of different size groups, some insights into the nature of the composite intermediation process of very large banks on the one hand and smaller banks on the other can be obtained from the data in Table 2-4.

For purposes of illustrating the composite intermediation process, assets are divided into five categories and liabilities into six categories. On the asset side the following summary comments on each category might be made:

1. Currency and due from banks. The major component here is legal reserve requirements. Operating cash needs are, of course, also included. Basic policy would always be to minimize this category to the extent consistent with legal and operating constraints; and at the minimum level this amount is essentially a nonliquid asset except in the very short run. This category might also include some discretionary acquisitions of large CDs from other banks in both domestic and Eurodollar markets, which functionally should appear in category (2) or (3).

2. Federal Funds sold and security resale agreements. These are earning assets with maturities for the most part of one day to a week or so. In large banks, a significant proportion represents dealer operations in the Federal Funds market and purchase of short-term funds of corporate customers under security resale agreements. In smaller banks, "Federal Funds sold" represents investment of excess reserves on a daily basis or the mechanism of implementing category (1) minimization policy. Both items may also be used as vehicles for liquidity or for funds awaiting investment in portfolio securities.

3. Portfolio securities. Four functional purposes may be associated with this category. (*a*) The trading account represents positions for implementing a broker-dealer operation in government securities, which is concentrated almost entirely in large banks. (*b*) Short maturities may function as a liquidity source, sometimes labeled as "secondary reserves." (*c*) The major function is either to implement spread management operations or to obtain

TABLE 2–4

Functional Uses and Sources of Funds:
Insured Commercial Banks
(In Billions of Dollars; as of 9/30/78)

Uses of Funds	Large Banks	Percent of Total	Other Banks	Percent of Total
(1) Currency and Due From Banks	41.3	8.2	48.0	7.4
(2) Federal Funds Sold and Security Resale Agreements	21.5	4.1	19.8	3.1
(3) Portfolio Securities:				
Trading account	6.4		.4	
U.S. Treasury and agency	40.3		89.9	
Municipals	39.1		80.8	
All other securities	1.3		4.0	
Total Securities	87.1	17.1	175.1	27.0
(4) Loans (Gross):				
Business loans*	170.1		123.5	
Real estate (includes construction loans)	65.9		137.5	
Loans to individuals	50.0		111.6	
All other loans	11.0		6.4	
Direct lease financing	5.2		1.5	
Total Loans	302.2	60.0	380.5	58.7
(5) Other Assets:				
Fixed assets	9.3		13.1	
Unconsolidated subsidiaries	3.2		—	
Customer acceptances	15.7		.9	
Nonclassified	25.1		10.8	
Total Other Assets	53.3	10.5	24.8	3.8
Total Uses of Funds	505.4	100.0	648.2	100.0

(Continues)

Table 2-4 *(Continued)*

Sources of Funds	Large Banks	Percent of Total	Other Banks	Percent of Total
(1) Core Deposits:				
Demand (gross)	177.4		191.6	
Less: items in process				
of collection	55.6		13.5	
Net collected demand deposits	121.8		178.1	
Retail savings and time deposits	109.4		289.8	
Total Core Deposits	231.2	45.8	476.9	73.6
(2) Purchased Funds:				
Large certificates of deposit				
($100,000 or more)	111.2		72.4	
Short-term borrowing				
(Fed Funds, etc.)	78.8		21.9	
Total Purchased Funds	190.0	37.7	94.3	14.6
(3) Long-Term Borrowings	1.0	—	.8	—
(4) Contra Items:				
Acceptances outstanding	15.7		.9	
Unearned income on loans	4.5		12.5	
Loan loss reserve	3.9		3.5	
Total Contra items	24.1	4.8	16.9	2.6
(5) Nonclassified Liabilities	19.1	3.8	8.0	1.3
(6) Capital Accounts:				
Subordinated debt	3.1		2.7	
Equity capital	36.9		48.6	
Total Capital	40.0	7.9	51.3	7.9
Total Sources of Funds	505.4	100.0	648.2	100.0

*Includes loans to financial institutions, security dealers and brokers, farm loans, and commercial and industrial loans.

returns on core funds not required for other purposes. (*d*) Some municipals essentially represent loans to local governments that are regular customers of the banks; in this instance acquisition may not necessarily occur on a strictly impersonal basis.

4. Loans. This category represents the major use of bank funds. The loan portfolio has two principal components: (*a*) commercial loans to regular business customers, including agricultural, trade, manufacturing, and service industries; and (*b*) "retail" loans, which include mortgages, installment loans, and bank credit card usage. The latter two are shown as "loans to individuals." Note that such loans dominate the loan accounts of smaller banks, but they are also of significant size in large banks.

5. *Other assets.* This category consists largely of the facilities required to conduct banking business (fixed assets and investment in unconsolidated subsidiaries), or result from accounting conventions (accruals under "non-classified" assets). Claims against customers for acceptances are an offset to the liability for outstanding acceptances, wherein the credit of the bank is substituted for the credit of the customer or for foreign trade transactions.

The liability side of the position statement is comprised largely of the sources of bank funds. Six functional categories may be identified.

1. *Core deposits.* In the format of Table 2–4, demand deposits are shown net of "items in process of collection," which technically are an asset but in reality represent the amount of demand deposits credited to customers' accounts which are not yet available for intermediation into earning assets. Retail savings and time deposits are those of denominations less than $100,000; most are subject to Reg Q rate limits, although six-month money market certificates of $10,000 or more tied to Treasury bill rates are also included here.[7] Note that demand deposits constitute a relatively larger proportion of total core deposits in large banks than in smaller banks.

2. *Purchased funds.* This category includes all funds exempt from Reg Q and thus presumably acquired at competitive rates in the market. As noted in the table, the CDs must have a minimum denomination of $100,000 and a minimum maturity of thirty days. Some may be acquired to accommodate customers, but most are probably purchased on a discretionary competitive-bid basis. Rates paid on these funds may differ to a moderate degree because of perceived differences in the soundness of various banks. Short-term borrowings include purchases of Federal Funds to implement dealer operations as well as discretionary acquisitions for liquidity needs or for spread banking operations.

Purchased funds, therefore, may have several functional purposes: (*a*) to provide a source of funds to meet liquidity needs on core deposits and loan programs; (*b*) to provide a source of funds to implement spread management operations; (*c*) to accommodate customers; and (*d*) to implement dealer operations in Federal Funds, an operation which requires willing-

---

7. For purposes of estimating sources of funds related to the current level of interest rates, a breakout of money market certificates would be highly desirable. As of the end of 1979, however, published data on the banking system did not provide this breakout.

ness to acquire or sell such funds at prevailing rates from those using the dealer service on a regular basis.

3. Long-term borrowing. These represent a relatively minor source of funds to banks and are probably obtained for the most part to finance fixed assets. This category is therefore incidental in nature and not considered an integral part of the financial intermediation process.

4. Contra items. The largest proportion of this category, as noted above, is the bank's liability under acceptances, which in essence is a contra to the customer obligation on these acceptances. Unearned income and the loan loss reserve are essentially contra accounts to the loan portfolio. In most published statements of condition these items are deducted from the total amount of loans.

5. Nonclassified liabilities. This category is not further defined by the data source, but it might be conjectured that it includes accruals, such as income tax liabilities, and other liabilities resulting from accounting conventions designed to match periodic income and expenses. Only technically, therefore, can this category be considered a source of funds; for the most part it should probably be construed as a contra to the "other asset" accounts.

6. Capital accounts. Shareholder equity constitutes by far the greatest proportion of this category, although some banks have issued long-term debt which becomes capital if the claim is subordinated to depositors and other creditors. Shareholder equity includes the capital stock account (par value), surplus, and undivided profits, which in total represent the book value of the outstanding shares. The functions of capital are (*a*) to provide funds for bank facilities and other permanent operating assets, (*b*) to create confidence in customers and the regulatory authorities that temporary adversity can be absorbed without difficulty, and (*c*) to provide a margin of protection for creditors in the event of financial difficulties.

The regulatory authorities evaluate the capital position of a bank both during examinations and when the bank or the associated holding company requests permission for additional branches or new activities. Regulatory guidelines for capital adequacy are expressed in part in terms of the relationship of capital to total assets and to risk assets (defined as total assets less cash and government obligations). The capital position of a bank, therefore, may limit the total amount of other funds that may be prudently intermediated into earning assets. As an extensive and somewhat controversial body of literature exists on capital adequacy evaluation,[8] this facet of bank management will not be further examined in this book.

8. Cf. G. H. Hempel, *Bank Capital: Determining and Meeting Your Bank's Capital Needs* (Boston: Bankers Publishing Company, 1976), pp. 1–100.

3

LIQUIDITY MANAGEMENT

Given the assumption that funds management must accommodate cash flow variations in both the loan portfolio and core deposits, it is axiomatic that liquidity policies designed to meet these flows should have a high managerial priority. Inability to meet depositor demands results in severe regulatory action at best and failure at worst, and it may be presumed that loan programs must be funded on a reasonably consistent basis for a bank to remain competitive in its markets.[1]

Policies designed to assure adequate liquidity represent a major constraint on funds management operations aimed at long-term earnings maximization. The constraint may operate on both the configuration of the investment portfolio and the amounts and structure of the purchased funds position. In some banks, funds management policies may also be constrained by problems of capital adequacy. As mentioned earlier, however, assessment of capital adequacy is a highly complex and controversial issue. Moreover, the appropriate remedy is usually either a reappraisal of the dividend payout ratio or perhaps the issuance of some form of subordinated long-term debt or equity securities (or a combination thereof) at irregular time intervals. In brief, our assumption is that capital considerations do not represent a major permanent constraint on asset and liability management policies.[2]

1. Regulatory examinations include assessment of liquidity policies as a major feature of the examination process, and security analysts typically compare the liquidity status of publicly owned banks and holding companies as part of their analysis. In May of 1978 the three federal bank regulatory agencies (Federal Reserve, Comptroller of the Currency, and FDIC), announced a new uniform system for rating the condition of banks. Appraisal of the liquidity position was listed as one of "five critical aspects of a bank's operation and condition." Federal Reserve Bank of New York, "A New Supervisory System for Rating Banks," *Quarterly Review,* Summer 1978, p. 47.

2. In smaller banks that have limited access to the capital markets and are also growing rapidly, capital adequacy may be a chronic and serious problem which slants the configuration of the investment portfolio toward low risk assets well beyond those needed for liquidity purposes. We regard this situation as a special case rather than a general phenomenon.

Dimensions of liquidity

Statistical analysis of time series data conventionally divides the sequence of temporal variations into four categories: (1) short-term random movements, (2) intrayear seasonal movements, (3) cyclical variations over one to several years, and (4) long-term growth trends over five to ten years or so. Because the time series properties of core deposits and loans are the essential determinants of liquidity requirements, it is convenient to appraise liquidity needs and related policies according to these conventional time series identifications. Only the growth property would not be relevant to liquidity analysis, as presumably all asset and liability components, including loan programs, would necessarily adjust to the long-term trends of the service area on a gradual basis. Of the remaining three categories, cyclical variations are by far the most important in terms of severity of impact on earnings and possibly on the fundamental soundness of the bank as a going concern. The major concern of this chapter, therefore, is to discuss the policy options available for managing liquidity pressures resulting from cyclical monetary restraint policies imposed in recent years to limit strong inflationary surges in the economy.

Money position management

Random or irregular short-term fluctuations in deposits and loans are adjusted through the cash reserve accounts. Because the expectation is that they will fluctuate around a zero mean, the adjustment process is designed to optimize the cash reserve position through time. A basic axiom of efficient banking is that cash reserves ("cash and due from banks") should be monitored daily, if not hourly, to keep the amount at the minimum consistent with operating needs (such as teller window cash), legal reserve requirements, and tacit understandings with correspondent banks rendering services in exchange for deposit balances. The reason, of course, is that these assets for the most part provide no earnings.[3]

Operating needs for vault cash and correspondent balances can be assumed to be essentially fixed amounts, except for special or nonrecurring reasons such as an increase in the number of branches or an augmentation of correspondent services. In contrast, because net daily cash flows due to deposit and loan fluctuations are usually settled through the deposit account at the Federal Reserve, the daily layoff of net inflows to or replenishment of net outflows from this account is a routine part of funds management. In the jargon of banking this is known as "managing the money position."

3. The qualification of the nonearning status of a part of the "due from banks" account is necessary because on a purely discretionary basis, CDs of other banks are among the options for short-term liquid earning assets. Such holdings are shown in the "cash and due from banks" account. Also, legislative proposals which will allow interest payments on demand deposits and on legal reserves held at the Federal Reserve are pending. If these proposals become law, they would modify these policy objectives to some extent.

Members of the Federal Reserve System manage their reserve positions in accordance with Regulation D. In essence, this regulation prescribes that *average* daily legal reserves for "computation" periods of one week's duration must meet the minimum percentage requirements prescribed for various categories of deposits for *average* daily levels of such deposits during a prior period.[4] This means that the average reserve target for a given computation period is known in advance, but the actual reserves held on any given day can be either below or above the target amount. Daily deficiencies or excesses are accumulated and appropriate adjustments are made as necessary either during or at the end of the computation period.

The hypothetical example given in Table 3-1 might be useful to demonstrate the adjustment process options. Here it is assumed that the average daily legal reserve target for a computation period of five days is $5 million and net deposit and loan inflows and outflows result in a sequence of re-

TABLE 3-1

Management of Legal Reserve Position
(Hypothetical Example; $5,000,000 Average Daily Requirements)

	Day 1	Day 2	Day 3	Day 4	Day 5
Reserves Held	4,000,000	5,500,000	4,800,000	5,100,000	5,600,000*
Daily Deficiency	(1,000,000)	—	(200,000)	—	—
Daily Excess	—	500,000	—	100,000	600,000
Accumulated Deficiency or Excess	(1,000,000)	(500,000)	(700,000)	(600,000)	-0-

*This level is required on day 5 and can be reached by appropriate borrowing if necessary.

serve deficiencies or excesses of varying amounts over the first four days. The data sequence in Table 3-1 suggests the first management option: allow the daily inflows and outflows to accumulate until the end of the settlement period and then purchase or sell sufficient reserves on the final day to even out the position. The problem with this option is that Fed Fund rates are highly unpredictable on the final day of a computation period because supply and demand for Fed Funds on that day depend on the net accumulated excess and deficiency positions in the entire system. Thus, on Wednesday of each week (the final day of each computation period), it is not uncommon for Fed Fund rates to average as much as 500 basis points above or below the average rate for the week and to fluctuate widely during the day.

4. Board of Governors of the Federal Reserve System, *Regulation D,* Section 204.3, July 6, 1978.

A second option is to even out the position on a daily basis. This would mean that on the first day Fed Funds would be purchased (or any existing position in "Fed Funds sold" reduced) in the amount necessary to eliminate the deficiency. Thereafter, daily adjustments would be made to keep the actual reserves at the target requirement. Use of this option results in two benefits: the average yields of Fed Funds are obtained and the uncertainties associated with the settlement day are largely eliminated. Moderate-sized banks tend to use this option as a normative policy, and many smaller banks continuously maintain a positive "Fed Funds sold" position which varies to accommodate short-term random fluctuations in deposits and loan demands.

A third option is to acquire or sell more funds on a given day or series of days than are actually required to balance out a position because rates for those days are considered more attractive than the rates forecasted for subsequent days. This option seems most feasible for relatively large banks that conduct dealer operations in the Fed Funds market, and which as a consequence are able to evaluate the short-term nuances of the market on a continuous basis. However, in October of 1979 the Federal Reserve announced that it was deemphasizing control of the Fed Funds rate as a means of implementing monetary policy. This step presumably means that Fed Funds rates may fluctuate over a much wider daily and weekly range than previously had been tolerated. As a consequence, the risks associated with large trading positions in Fed Funds have necessarily increased, and the result may be more conservative policies with respect to operations in this market.

Table 3–2 shows the policy preferences of the respondent banks in managing short-term random variations in deposits and loans. The Fed Funds market was clearly the dominant adjustment mechanism used, although a minority of smaller banks showed a reluctance to assume a net Fed Funds purchased position. Repos (to acquire funds) or reverse repos (to lay off funds) were generally considered a normative option for short-term funds management by large banks, but fewer than half of the banks with assets of less than $1 billion included this instrument as an option. The likely reason is that only large customers are familiar with the repurchase agreement process and many smaller banks have few, if any, such customers.

Only a few banks cited direct borrowings from the Federal Reserve as a regular source of short-term funds. The greater convenience of the Fed Funds market and the penchant of the Fed to disapprove of regular borrowings make this source of funds exceptional rather than normative.[5]

---

5. When the Fed discount rate is significantly below the Fed Funds rate, which happens from time to time, the popularity of direct borrowings from the Fed to manage short-term liquidity needs seems to increase significantly. And, as will be mentioned below, some

TABLE 3-2

Use of Various Liquidity Sources for Managing
Short-Term Random Fluctuations
(Respondent Banks; by Size Groups

| | Amount of Assets (in Millions of Dollars) | | | | | |
| | To 300 | | 300–1,000 | | Over 1,000 | |
	Yes	No	Yes	No	Yes	No
Source (Regular):						
Federal Funds sold	12	—	13	—	9	—
Federal Funds purchased	8	4	12	1	9	—
Repurchase agreements*	4	6	5	7	8	1
Others Given:						
Federal Reserve window	1		2		—	
Eurodollar purchases and sales	—		—		5	

*These are formally "sales of securities with agreement to repurchase" where the bank sells marketable securities (usually governments) to a customer with a legal obligation to repurchase the securities after a specified time interval, usually a few days to a week or so.

Finally, more than half of the large banks regularly used the Eurodollar market as a short-term adjustment option. It may be presumed that only those with direct access to this market in London would use this source on a regular basis, but given such access the comparative costs or yields on funds in the several alternative markets will determine the actual option used at a given time.

Seasonal liquidity management

Banks vary widely as to seasonal needs for liquidity. At one extreme are those banks located in agricultural or tourist areas where seasonal cash flow patterns may dominate the entire liquidity management process. For example, one respondent offered the following comment:

...we are located in a tourist area, thus have large...deposit flows and as a result [we] have a line of credit [at the Federal Reserve] up to $10,500,000 for a seven-month period. It requires careful planning plus Federal Reserve [seasonal] borrowing privilege. This [privilege] is a *very* big item...for country banks with seasonal deposit and loan flows of unusual magnitude.

At the other extreme are banks located in areas with a highly diversified economic base which report no discernible seasonal pattern in their core

moderate-sized banks with major seasonal variations in deposits and loans, primarily in agricultural and tourist areas, take advantage of a seasonal borrowing line at the Federal Reserve. Because the Fed has experienced problems in holding small state banks in the system, the liberalization of the borrowing privilege may be extended even further.

deposits and loan demand. Of the respondent universe of thirty-five banks, five (14 percent) indicated no seasonal liquidity needs. Intuitively, one might expect these to be large banks, but as shown in Table 3-3, three were in the category of banks having assets of less than $300 million.

Because seasonal variations tend to be repetitive in extent, duration, and timing, forecasts of requirements based on time series data of past experience should have a reasonably high confidence factor. Therefore, there would seem to be only moderate risk associated with the use of purchased funds to cover seasonal liquidity needs because there should be a very high probability that subsequent net cash inflows will provide the funds for repayment. The positive results of such a policy are that loan program targets and the investment portfolios can then be structured on the basis of fund availability at seasonal highs in core deposits. Assuming an opportunity cost sacrifice in the form of lower average yields on liquid assets (secondary reserves) relative to average returns on investment portfolio assets, earnings maximization would be achieved through a policy structured to manage seasonal liquidity with purchased funds.

The empirical evidence derived from the respondent banks shows that the majority of banks do manage seasonal liquidity requirements through short-term borrowings. As shown in Table 3-3, eighteen of the thirty banks with a seasonal liquidity problem indicated that some form of short-term borrowings represented their first priority in this connection. However, ten still held to the traditional policy of using secondary reserve type assets, and it is notable that two moderate-sized banks relied exclusively on asset liquidation to manage seasonal requirements. Thus, it appears that even the policy of handling routine seasonal liquidity requirements through liability management techniques is far from universal in the banking system.

Finally, it should be mentioned that large CDs did not represent the preferred vehicle for managing seasonal liquidity. The reason is that nondeposit borrowings offer lower normative costs and greater maturity flexibility.

Cyclical Liquidity Management

Empirical experience: 1969-79

During the years 1969 to 1979 inclusive, funds management policies received their greatest challenge since the Great Depression of 1930-35. The challenge, in essence a consequence of the cyclical behavior of the economy, had several dimensions. First, in 1974-75 certain major loan sectors encountered credit losses well beyond any previous postwar experience. Second, the upper parameters of interest rates resulting from successive phases of severe monetary restraint moved well above historical precedents. Third, in 1970 and again in 1974, as interest rates moved much higher than rate limits imposed by Regulation Q, core deposits declined or became inadequate to fund loan demand. In 1979, however, the rapid growth of money market certificates greatly reduced disintermediation

TABLE 3-3

Seasonal Liquidity Management Policies
(Respondent Banks; by Size Groups)

	Amount of Assets (in Millions of Dollars)		
	To 300*†‡	300–1,000§	Over 1,000
Seasonal Variations Expected:			
Yes	10	13	7
No	3	—	2
Funding Preferences for Seasonal Variations:			
Fed Funds purchased			
Priority 1	5	7	3
Priority 2	1	3	3
Priority 3	—	1	—
Priority 4	—	1	1
Repos			
Priority 1	1	—	2
Priority 2	—	3	2
Priority 3	2	3	2
Priority 4	2	6	1
Large CDs			
Priority 1	—	—	—
Priority 2	3	5	2
Priority 3	2	6	5
Priority 4	—	1	—
Asset liquidation			
Priority 1	3	5	2
Priority 2	1	1	—
Priority 3	1	2	—
Priority 4	2	4	5

*One bank with assets of less than $300 million used the Federal Reserve seasonal borrowing privilege exclusively for seasonal liquidity requirements.

†Two banks with assets of less than $300 million relied exclusively on asset liquidation to handle seasonal needs.

‡One bank with assets of less than $300 million used Fed Funds exclusively for seasonal needs. No other priority was indicated.

§One bank with assets of $300 to $1,000 million responded that it had no priority policies for handling seasonal needs. Ad hoc decisions apparently are made each year.

problems, but greatly increased the cost and volatility of the liability universe.

Table 3-4 shows that the range of interest rate fluctuations clearly departed from historical precedents after 1968, particularly in 1973–74 and again in 1978–79. (Average figures for 1961–67 are given for purposes of comparison.) Based on precedents, the parameter in early 1969 for a "high" in short-term rates may have been on the order of 7 percent. An asset allocation model based on the strong presumed probability of decline from such levels might well have dictated the acquisition of extended maturity assets with purchased funds (CDs). Yet in the next year and a half this policy would have proved disastrous, as short-term rates moved above 9 percent.

Then, after interest rates declined significantly in 1971–72, the subsequent cyclical peak on CDs was 12.6 percent in 1974, once again well above the previous high. Again, a forecast probability distribution based on historical experience would have been seriously in error within a few years. Aggressive acquisitions of long-term obligations to lock in the high rates prevailing at the end of 1973 would at that time have seemed entirely logical; but for most of 1974 both the cost and availability of purchased funds

TABLE 3-4

Selected Short-Term Interest Rates
(Yearly Range of Monthly Averages; 1968–79)

| | Three-Month Maturities | | | | | |
| | Treasury Bills | | Prime CDs | | Eurodollars | |
	Low	High	Low	High	Low	High
1968	4.9%	5.7%	5.2%	6.1%	5.4%	7.4%
1969	6.0	7.5	6.4	8.8	7.1	11.3
1970	5.4	7.7	5.3	9.0	7.1	9.8
1971	3.4	5.3	4.0	5.8	5.3	9.0
1972	3.4	4.9	3.8	5.3	4.9	5.9
1973	5.1	8.7	5.6	10.9	5.8	11.5
1974	6.2	10.0	8.1	12.6	8.6	13.9
1975	5.2	7.1	5.6	9.1	6.0	10.1
1976	4.7	5.2	4.9	6.0	5.3	6.6
1977	4.3	6.2	4.7	6.7	5.0	7.2
1978	6.1	9.3	6.8	10.9	7.2	12.2
1979*	9.3	12.5	10.0	14.5	10.3	15.4
1961–67	2.2	5.3	2.9	5.9	3.4	7.1

Source: Salomon Brothers, *An Analytical Record of Yields and Spreads,* Part IV, Table 1.

*Highs for 1979 are estimated on the basis of highs registered through October.

became increasingly difficult problems. As a consequence, some banks were obliged to incur significant losses on security liquidations during that year when their liquidity sources became inadequate.

Until late in 1979 most money market rates did not exceed their 1974 highs, but the duration of the restraint period had already been well in excess of previous episodes. Because Regulation Q constraints were relaxed in this period, mainly through the authorization of money market certificates pegged to the six-month Treasury bill rate, disintermediation of core deposits was not a serious problem for most banks. As a consequence, liquidity management policies became increasingly oriented to the issue of maintaining yield spreads rather than to the funding of deposit declines and loan increases, which had been the major problems associated with preceding restraint periods. Savings and time deposits subject to Regulation Q limits were replaced in large amounts by high-cost money market certificates, and indeed the marginal costs of these funds exceeded the yields on several types of retail loans subject to regulatory rate maximums. Maintaining a competitive posture in the retail loan markets requires reasonable consistency in terms; the policy issue therefore became the means of funding these programs at tolerable cost levels. However, the rapid rise of interest costs on CDs and money market certificates necessarily had a serious effect on the earnings of those banks that had not maintained an adequate amount of interest-sensitive assets, and at the end of 1979 a number of banks felt obliged to take the drastic step of curtailing retail loan programs, particularly mortgages.

The effects of the monetary restraint policies on the respondent banks during 1974 and 1978 are shown in Table 3–5. About 45 percent of the banks indicated that in the former period an increase in loan demand was associated with an absolute decline in core deposits. Most of the remainder indicated that even though attempts were made to restrain some loan programs, total loans still increased at a more rapid rate than core deposits. Disintermediation of time and savings deposits subject to Regulation Q rate limits was thus the principal cause of the sluggish deposit performance.

At the same time, loan demand actually increased in many banks due to the combination of accelerating inflation and the delayed effect of the restraint policies on business activity. Unfortunately, the data in Table 3–5 do not reflect the impact of events in late 1979 when the Fed made a significant change in monetary policy tactics. But fragmentary evidence suggests that although loan demand remained strong because of the new money market certificates, core deposit growth in total was sufficient in most cases to require only moderate asset liquidation or additional use of purchased funds. Therefore, as noted above, the nature of the liquidity problem largely changed from one of *amount* (funding a combination of deposit declines and loan growth) to one of *cost* (finding means of improving asset

TABLE 3-5

Effects of Monetary Restraint, 1974 and 1978
(Respondent Banks; by Size Groups)

	Amount of Assets (in Millions of Dollars)		
	To 300 (N = 13)	300–1,000 (N = 13)	Over 1,000 (N = 9)
Type of Effect:			
Decline in core deposits	3	7	5
Loan increase exceeds core deposit increase	8	11	8
Reduced margin of core deposit increase relative to loan increase	2	–	1
No apparent effect	1	1	–

Note: Some banks listed more than one effect, indicating differential effects of monetary restraint in the two periods. Data include all effects listed.

yields to match the rapidly escalating costs of the greater proportion of deposits based on short-term interest rates in the market).

This new dimension of liquidity management will probably become dominant in the future, as it can be expected that the proportion of deposits controlled by Regulation Q limits will gradually decline. As a consequence, policies for management of the interest-sensitivity position will probably become increasingly important relative to traditional liquidity policies, which were largely concerned with providing adequate amounts of funds to meet deposit outflows and/or loan increases under conditions of monetary restraint.

The impact of the unprecedented levels and volatility of short-term interest rates in late 1979 has yet to be reflected in the empirical results of the banking universe. Except for the few purely wholesale banks where practically the entire asset universe is interest-sensitive, the effects on earnings should be negative, but if the 1974–75 experience can be used as a guide, the differential impact will probably vary widely.

In 1974–75, the decline in net interest margins consequent to excessive use of purchased funds to meet liquidity needs resulted in a significant erosion of the earnings of some banks. At the same time, however, a large proportion of banks showed significant improvements in earnings. Table 3–6 indicates the wide dispersion of earnings results in the banking industry for the recession year of 1975. As all banks were subject to the same exogenous circumstances, it seems quite remarkable that of a sample of publicly owned banks, some 30 percent suffered earnings declines of 10 percent or more in 1975 while another 27 percent enjoyed earnings increases of 10 percent or more.[6] Some of the variations may have been due to different cyclical exposures in the various geographic service areas. But as larger banks usually extend their services over fairly wide geographic regions, it seems more probable that differences in liquidity management policies and possibly loan losses were the primary causes of the diverse results.

TABLE 3-6

Commercial Banks: 1975 Earnings Results
(Percentage Changes Compared to 1974; Sample of 126 Banks)

	Number	% of Total
Decrease in Earnings:		
Over 30%	20	15.8
20-29%	7	5.6
10-19%	11	8.7
0-9%	13	10.4
Total decreases	51	40.5
Increase in Earnings:		
Over 30%	6	4.8
20-29%	3	2.4
10-19%	25	19.8
0-9%	41	32.5
Total increases	75	59.5

Source: Wall Street Journal, Jan. 5-28, 1976.

As a consequence of this experience, the 1978 Uniform Interagency Bank Rating System established new criteria for evaluating the liquidity positions of banks. In view of the 1979 liquidity "cost crunch," they would seem highly appropriate as guidelines to bank management in establishing liquidity policies:

> Among the factors in evaluating liquidity are the availability of assets readily convertible into cash, the bank's formal and informal commitments for future lending or investment, the structure and volatility of deposits, the reliance on interest-sensitive funds including money market instruments and other sources of borrowing, and the ability to adjust rates on loans when rates on interest-sensitive sources of funds fluctuate. The examiner-analyst will review the frequency and level of borrowings and include judgments of the bank's ability to sustain any level of borrowings over the business cycle or to attract new sources of funds.[7]

---

6. The sample is biased toward larger banks as the *Wall Street Journal* does not publish earnings for small banks with limited markets for their securities.

7. Federal Reserve Bank of New York, "New Supervisory System," p. 50.

Cyclical liquidity: policy issues

In view of the empirical experience of the past decade, it is clear that liquidity policies should be structured to accomplish two ends: (1) to provide sources of funds to meet possible deposit declines and/or increased customer loan demands and, probably of more importance, (2) to control the interest-sensitivity position (defined as the amount and ratio of interest-sensitive assets to interest-sensitive liabilities). Policies of the first type are entirely defensive in nature, as their purposes are to avoid competitive disruption of loan programs, ensure the perception of "soundness" on the part of both fund providers and users, and—in the worst case—avoid drastic regulatory reactions.

Interest-sensitivity policies, however, are partly defensive and partly positive. Their defensive (liquidity) purpose, which is undoubtedly most important, is to avoid serious earnings problems consequent to major fluctuations in short-term interest rate levels. However, on the positive side, there may be a secondary purpose: to manage the sensitivity position in order to increase average net interest margins based on yield curve relationships and expectations for changes in interest rates. Since these objectives of interest-sensitivity management are interdependent, both aspects will be considered in the chapter on spread management policies.

Liquidity sources

Table 3–7 shows the policies of respondent banks with respect to sources of funds considered appropriate to meet potential cyclical variations in deposits and loans. At one extreme, two banks indicated that they relied entirely on liquid assets. At the opposite extreme, two moderate-sized banks held no asset secondary reserves to provide liquidity during periods of monetary restraint.[8]

The policy of the great majority, however, was to use both assets and liabilities as liquidity sources, although significant differences in policy constraints existed within the liability universe. By a slight margin, the sale of CDs to customers was the preferred liability source, followed closely by short-term borrowings. Only the largest banks had a positive policy toward obtaining CD funds from noncustomers on a competitive-bid basis. The smaller banks were split on the issue: the majority rejected this source of funds and others indicated sporadic or last resort usage only.

Finally, the greatest policy difference between large banks and those of moderate size was with respect to the use of brokered CDs (impersonal sale through investment dealers). Although it was not unanimous, large banks

8. It should be noted that these two banks also indicated that liquidity requirements under monetary restraint conditions had not been of serious proportions in either 1974 or 1978.

TABLE 3-7

Monetary Restraint Liquidity Management
(Respondent Banks; by Size Groups)

| | Amount of Assets (in Millions of Dollars) | | | | | |
| | To 300 | | 300–1,000 | | Over 1,000 | |
	Yes	No	Yes	No	Yes	No
Secondary Reserves Held	12	—	11	2	9	—
Liability Usage:						
Short-term borrowings	10	2	10	3	8	1
Large CDs:						
To customers	10	2	11	2	9	—
To noncustomers	5	7	5	8	8	1
To investment dealers	1	11	—	13	7	2

generally regarded dealer-placed CDs as an acceptable source of funds. However, with one exception, all respondents with assets of less than $1 billion had a negative policy regarding their use. Two reasons for the negative posture might be cited. First, if a bank does not have national visibility in the financial markets, then regardless of its intrinsic soundness, a significant rate premium is required on brokered CD sales.[9] Second, the reliability of these funds may be questioned, particularly during peak periods of monetary restraint when CD buyers may become highly selective on fund placements. Given these properties of the CD market, only large banks can appropriately rely on funds acquired through dealer placements as a cyclical liquidity source.

Usage options

Although some specific liability categories were considered unacceptable, it is clear that most banks, even those of moderate size, have a positive policy of using both asset and liability sources in their liquidity management. Given the alternative options, tactical decisions are required as to which funding methods will be relatively favored under a given set of dynamic endogenous and exogenous circumstances. Several cost and risk factors were listed and respondents were requested to indicate which, if any, were applicable to management decisions. The hypothesized factors and the banks within each group that considered each factor applicable to their decisions are shown in Table 3-8.

9. D. D. Crane, "A Study of Interest Rate Spreads in the 1974 CD Market," *Journal of Bank Research,* Autumn 1976, p. 215.

TABLE 3-8

Monetary Restraint Liquidity Management
Cost and Risk Factors
(Respondent Banks; by Size Groups)

	Amount of Assets (in Millions of Dollars)		
	To 300	300-1,000	Over 1,000
	(N = 10)*	(N = 11)*	(N = 9)
Cost Factors			
Cost of purchased funds compared to book yields on assets considered for sale	5	9	5
Cost of purchased funds compared to market yield on assets considered for sale	7	5	9
Perceived ability to incur losses on sale of assets	9	9	9
Risk Factors			
Perceived reliability of purchased funds	5	11	8
Policy limits on purchased funds	6	11	5
Need to constrain total risk asset position	6	7	7
Other factors mentioned:			
Interest rate sensitivity gap target			
Perceived closeness of interest rates to cyclical peak			

*Two banks in each of these groups were excluded because they did not use *both* assets and liabilities to meet liquidity needs.

On the cost side, accounting conventions and tax considerations may complicate the decision. In the absence of these factors, the cost of providing the necessary liquidity would be minimized by a comparison of the market yields on assets considered for sale with the interest cost of the purchased funds (adjusted for reserve requirements and FDIC assessment if deposit CDs). By way of illustration, assume the following asset data:

Cost base	100
Yield on cost	7%
Market price	90

Yield on market   11%
Cost of purchased funds   10%

Under these conditions the sale of the asset at 90 represents an opportunity cost of 11 percent, as that is the return available on the security at that price; indeed, using purchased funds to acquire the asset would yield a spread profit of 1 percent. Large banks, perhaps because of their greater sophistication in spread operations compared to smaller banks, showed a distinct preference for using market yield rather than book yield (cost base) as the basis for determining comparative costs.

But the security sale would minimize the impact on reported operating earnings before security gains and losses, because income recognition on the asset for this purpose is only 7 percent and the opportunity cost impact is 7.8 percent (7 ÷ 90). Moreover, if the bank has taxable earnings from other sources against which the loss on the sale can be deducted, then the tax savings decrease the true cost of the asset sale. A rough adjustment for the tax effect can be calculated by adding the tax savings to the market price of the asset and computing the yield on the "tax adjusted" market price, which is then compared to the cost of purchased funds.

However, if it is perceived that discretionary security losses would excessively reduce reported net income, then purchased funds rather than asset sales might be the tactical choice. On the other hand, if taxable earnings for the year are above goal expectations, then the perceived ability to absorb security losses becomes high, and a preference for asset sales would result.[10] In addition, sale of long-dated securities to fund liquidity requirements may also be desirable to reach or maintain interest-sensitivity targets. Several banks specifically mentioned this factor as relevant to their tactical decisions.

The hypothesized risk factors relate solely to the purchased funds option, and it is clear that risk perceptions are of considerable significance in tactical decisions about their usage. All but one of the twenty respondent banks with assets over $300 million agreed that the perceived reliability of these funds could constrain their use as a liquidity source, and a significant majority indicated that formal policy limits on purchased funds also represent a restraining factor. As mentioned above, a large proportion of these funds is obtained on a relatively impersonal basis from a sophisticated universe of buyers (other banks in the case of Fed Funds, and corporations and governmental units in the case of CDs or repos). Moreover, FDIC deposit

10. Although theoretical arguments can be advanced that the practice is not entirely rational, both shareholders and security analysts seem to place a high value on consistent growth in reported earnings. Therefore, there is considerable incentive to make tactical asset/liability decisions with this objective in mind.

insurance covers only a fraction of their typical unit size. Consequently, most banks apparently hold the belief that excessive use could be subject to market constraints; indeed, past experience would support this position.[11]

Given risk constraints on the use of purchased funds to meet cyclical liquidity requirements, then logically an appropriate "reservoir" of purchased funds would be maintained under less stringent monetary conditions. The appropriate amount of the reservoir would be the difference between maximum estimated liquidity needs and the amount of reasonably liquid portfolio assets available for disposition. The planning model could be described as follows:

$$\text{Liquidity Position} = (\text{LA} - \text{LA}_{mi}) + [(\text{PF}_{mx} - \text{PF})(1 - \text{RR})]$$
$$\geq \text{Estimated Requirements, and}$$
$$\text{Estimated Requirements} = (\text{L}_{mx} - \text{L}) + [(\text{D} - \text{D}_{mi})(1 - \text{RR})],$$

where:

LA	= liquid assets now held,
LA_{mi}	= minimum tolerated liquid asset holdings,
PF_{mx}	= maximum purchased funds position,
PF	= existing purchased funds position,
RR	= average reserve requirements on mix of purchased funds (zero reserve requirements on borrowings),
L_{mx}	= maximum loans at peak cyclical demand,
L	= existing loans,
D	= existing core deposits, and
D_{mi}	= minimum expected core deposits.

The model makes the following assumptions:
1. A minimum amount of liquid assets would always be held for remote contingencies and "window dressing" purposes.
2. The maximum purchased funds position can be estimated.
3. Reserve requirements on the mix of purchased funds can be estimated.
4. The liquidity position should at least equal, and preferably should be moderately in excess of, estimated requirements.
5. Maximum loan demands are likely to be associated with minimum

---

11. In 1970, the Commonwealth Bank in Detroit was known to be using purchased funds in large amounts, and a public letter from the Federal Reserve rejecting an application for an Edge Act Corporation led to a sudden shutdown of the bank's access to the Fed Funds and CD market. The result was serious difficulties which required massive injections of funds into the bank by the Fed and FDIC.

levels of core deposits under conditions of severe monetary restraint, and these amounts can be approximated.

It seems reasonable to assume that inflation will be a chronic problem. In addition, the Federal Reserve has specifically declared that monetary policy will focus increasingly on the behavior of the monetary aggregates rather than on "appropriate" interest rate levels. As a consequence, both a secular drift upward and continued high volatility in interest rates seem plausible outlooks for the future. Under these circumstances, optimal liquidity and interest-sensitivity management become very important to both continued soundness and earnings results.[12] The first policy priority, which has been the subject of this chapter, is to maintain adequate defensive liquidity. The next chapter will consider the second major issue in cyclical funds management: control of the interest-sensitivity position so as to produce reasonable stability in earnings despite probable continued turbulence in the financial markets.

12. An analysis of the earnings results of some large wholesale banks during the 1972–76 period indicated that cyclical funds management of some had been seriously deficient, and differences in overall performance were largely ascribed to this area of management. D. Cates, "Interest Sensitivity in Banks," *Bankers Magazine,* Jan.–Feb. 1978, pp. 23–27.

4

SPREAD MANAGEMENT

In a literal sense, interest spread management encompasses the entire financial intermediation function of banks. The possible exception to this generality is demand deposit intermediation where explicit interest costs are zero because of statutory prohibition. But as interest-bearing deposits and borrowings now heavily dominate the liability structure, it is reasonably accurate to view the intermediation process as acquiring funds at one set of interest rates and lending or investing them at another, with earnings results heavily dependent upon the difference between the two sets of rates. The major spread relationships can be shown as follows:

Interest Income[1]	$\div$	Earning Assets[2]	=	Asset yield rate
less				less
Interest costs	$\div$	Earning Assets	=	Asset cost rate
Net Interest Income				Net Interest Margin

Although banks incur other operating costs and derive noninterest income from other sources such as trust fees and service charges on demand deposit accounts, it has become increasingly evident that the behavior of

1. For comparative purposes interest income on tax-exempt securities is usually increased by dividing the actual interest received by a factor of (1 – Tax Rate) which assumes that the tax savings are in essence part of the interest yield on these securities as compared to others which are subject to taxes. The SEC, however, has taken the position that "the tax equivalency adjustment is not in accordance with generally accepted accounting principles but reflects theoretical income never actually realized by a company." Therefore, net interest income and a computed net interest margin derived therefrom, as shown in annual reports prepared in accordance with SEC requirements, cannot be used to compare results of various banks which may have materially different percentages of tax-exempt securities in their portfolios. Securities and Exchange Commission, *Accounting Series Release* 254, p. 2.

2. Total assets may also be used to show the effect on the yield rate of nonearning assets, mainly in the form of cash or equivalent, accruals, and physical facilities. It is, of course, desirable to show a high ratio of earning assets to total assets.

the net interest margin has become the most important determinant of earning performance. Reductions in net expense "burden" (defined as operating expenses other than interest costs less other income) as a percentage of assets may sometimes offer a moderate source of earnings improvement.[3] But managerial policies in this area are outside the scope of this study.[4]

An example of net interest margin analysis combined with "burden" analysis is shown in Table 4-1 for BankAmerica Corporation, the largest bank holding company in the United States. The results for this company indicate that a steady upward trend in net "burden" (adjusted for the cycli-

TABLE 4-1

BankAmerica Corporation:
Net Interest Margins and Expense "Burden" Analysis

Percentage of Average Earnings Assets	1973	1974	1975	1976
Taxable equivalent interest revenue	7.96%	10.44%	9.10%	8.40%
Interest expense	(5.21)	(7.42)	(5.83)	(5.23)
Taxable equivalent net interest revenue*	2.75%	3.02%	3.26%	3.18%
"Burden" items:†				
Personnel expenses	(1.23)	(1.30)	(1.32)	(1.42)
Other expenses	(0.85)	(0.97)	(1.03)	(0.97)
Loan loss provision	(0.15)	(0.27)	(0.38)	(0.27)
Noninterest revenue offset	0.80	0.73	0.74	0.74
Net "burden"	(1.43)	(1.81)	(1.99)	(1.92)
Taxable equivalent pretax profits	1.32%	1.21%	1.27%	1.26%

Source: BankAmerica Corporation, *Annual Report for 1976,* p. 54.

*Defined in text as "net interest margin."

†Term not used in data source; used here to illustrate text.

3. An analysis of banking industry data based on this "burden" concept showed that these expenses had increased greatly both as a percentage of assets and as a percentage of net income over the past several decades, and concluded that management will be forced to seek methods of improving productivity. It was also concluded that more effective asset/liability management techniques are required to offset the significant relative increases in "burden" over the years. J. V. Baker, "Why You Need a Formal Asset/Liability Management Policy," *Banking,* June 1978, p. 38.

4. The relative importance of net "burden," and thus the effects of management efforts to improve it, tends to vary with the nature of a bank's business. Retail banks, where installment and bankcard loans are a large proportion of earning assets, tend to have larger "burden" percentages because servicing costs absorb a larger fraction of the interest income on such loans than on commercial loans and investments. In those banks productivity improvements might be especially helpful in improving earnings.

cal variation in the loan loss provision) completely offset the improvement in net interest margins derived during those years.[5]

Because of an increase in leverage (a decline in the ratio of equity capital to total assets), the rate of return on equity showed a modest improvement. However, given probable regulatory constraints, this source of improvement in earnings performance might be construed as very limited; indeed, the upward shift in the leverage position between 1973 and 1975 was moderately reversed in the following two years.

The above analysis relates to the overall spread performance from all intermediation activities. But as discussed in Chapter 2, discretionary fund management policies cannot realistically be expected to control core deposit intermediation into loan programs except perhaps in a marginal way over an extended horizon. The scope of discretionary spread management, therefore, is limited to the management of those assets and liabilities that can be acquired and sold on an impersonal basis without regard to customer relationships. It also includes investment securities acquired with core deposits, if the amounts of such deposits exceed loan program requirements. The objectives, therefore, are (1) to achieve reasonable stability through time in the overall net interest margins and (2) to increase average net interest margins without unduly violating the first objective. A possible third objective is to insure that the total leverage position is maintained at target levels on both the low and the high sides. The assumption inherent in these objectives is that the amounts and maturities of impersonally acquired assets and sale of liabilities can vary to a considerable extent at the discretion of management.

Interest-Sensitivity Management

Interest-sensitivity management: defensive

The first of the above objectives is essentially defensive or protective in nature. Policies are structured and implemented so as to offset potential instability in the net interest margin arising from the expected dynamic behavior of core deposits and the loan portfolio through time. The goal is to manage effectively the interest-sensitivity position and estimated exposure so as to minimize the effects of fluctuations in interest rates on the net interest margin. The estimated exposure can be defined as a forecast of the interest-sensitivity position based on projected levels of pertinent assets and liabilities over a specified time horizon. The forecast estimation has the

---

5. In 1977 net interest margins improved again to a new high of 3.27 percent, but the annual report did not disclose the "burden" percentages. BankAmerica Corporation, *Annual Report for 1977*, p. 56.

following components: (1) the amount of existing assets whose rates will change during the specified time period; (2) the amount of existing liabilities similarly impacted; (3) the amounts of assets and liabilities now held that will become interest-sensitive because of the passage of time (for example, a bond with an existing maturity of one year is not currently interest-sensitive over a six-month time horizon but will become so six months from now); (4) the estimated changes in interest-sensitive and fixed-rate loans over the time period; and (5) the estimated changes in the amounts of various categories of the core deposit structure over the time period.

The first three components can be computed precisely over a specified time period. The relationship of the first two represents the interest-sensitivity position as of a given date, and can be computed as follows:
Interest-sensitive assets:
1. Floating-rate commercial loans,
2. Commercial loan maturities,
3. Investment portfolio maturities,[6] and possibly
4. Fixed-rate loan amortization.[7]
Interest-sensitive liabilities:
1. Short-term borrowings,
2. CD maturities,
3. Money market certificate maturities, and
4. Floating-rate liabilities (if any).

The last two components can be estimated only roughly at best because they depend on forecasts of future events wherein the margin of error may be extremely wide. For example, most banks probably have only an impressionistic perception of the amount of disintermediation of Reg Q-controlled deposits that is associated with specified levels of interest rates above ceiling rates or, vice versa, the rate of change in positive flows associated with declines in interest rates. The problem is to estimate the interest *elasticity* of such deposits (defined as the percentage change in their totals related to different levels of interest rates). In diagrammatic form, Figure

6. Includes Fed Funds sold, money market assets of all kinds, and all governments and municipals maturing within the time frame.

7. In theory such amortization is available for reallocation at current interest rate levels, but the normative policy to offer such loans on a consistent basis suggests that in reality the cash flows from amortization of fixed rate loans (mortgages, credit cards, and installment loans) will be reinvested in such loans. Therefore, only if a bank considers that such loan programs can be increased or decreased at will or firmly expects that demand for these loans will decrease, then and only then would loan portfolio amortization be considered interest-sensitive in nature. In reviewing the problem here, an otherwise excellent article on interest-sensitivity management first argues that loan amortization should be considered as interest-sensitive and then in a subsequent paragraph seems to reverse that position. J. V. Baker, "System Method of Asset/Liability Management: What It Is, How It Works," *Banking,* Sept. 1978, p. 124.

4–1 shows alternative hypothetical elasticity schedules on time and savings deposits limited to 5 percent maximum rates. Intuitively one would expect that the most important factor determining the shape of the interest elasticity schedule would be the size distribution of the universe. A universe where the average size is $5,000 is likely to be considerably more interest-elastic than one where the average size is $500. The reason is that the amount of additional income derived from transfer to higher yielding assets is relatively trivial on a $500 account ($15 per year more at 8 percent than at 5 percent) but becomes fairly substantial on a $5,000 account ($250 per year at 8 percent as compared to 5 percent).[8]

It is similarly very difficult to forecast the relative change in various loan categories over any significant time horizon, although past experience is probably a better guide here than in the case of deposits. As a result, the overall interest-sensitivity exposure of a bank can only be estimated in very general terms.

Nevertheless, a bank with a large proportion of its assets in fixed-rate retail loans funded largely with Reg Q-limited deposits might be well ad-

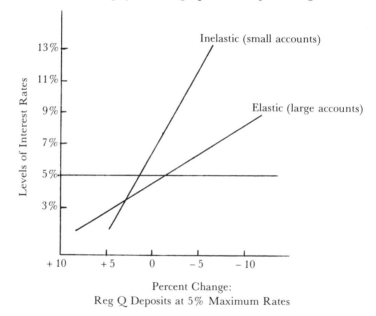

Fig 4–1. Hypothetical elasticity schedules (regulation Q-controlled deposits).

8. Because published data on the size distribution of the deposit universe are not available (indeed, most banks report that the information is not even available internally), verification of this hypothesis is not possible. However, in one bank in 1979, the disintermediation of a deposit category with a minimum entry size of $1,000 was significantly greater than a lower-yield category with no minimum entry size.

vised, for defensive reasons, to structure its discretionary funds management policy in such a way as to maintain a significant positive relationship between interest-sensitive assets and interest-sensitive liabilities. Table 4–2 shows the experience of one such bank during the last half of 1978 when interest rates increased well above Reg Q limits. These data clearly indicate the exposure of such banks to a significant, involuntary deterioration in their interest-sensitivity positions during periods when interest rates move

TABLE 4–2

Deposit and Loan Experience
(A Retail Bank; June–December 1978)

| | End-of-Month Position (in Millions of Dollars) | | |
	June	December	% Change
Savings and Time Deposits (Reg Q-limited)	$387.6	$366.8	– 7.2
Interest-Sensitive Deposits*	29.8	60.1	+ 101.7
Total	$417.4	$426.9	+ 2.2
Fixed-Rate Loans	$339.8	$359.7	+ 5.9
Floating-Rate Loans	67.2	65.1	– 3.1
Total	$407.0	$424.8	+ 4.4

*Includes large CDs and money market certificates first authorized at beginning of June 1978.

well above Reg Q maximums and demands for loans in the retail sectors remain strong. In the case of this particular bank, the decline in Reg Q-controlled deposits in combination with a significant increase in fixed-rate loans produced a funding requirement that necessarily had to be met through additional interest-sensitive funds. The result was that the margin between interest-sensitive loans and interest-sensitive deposits declined by more than $32 million. Inevitably, these developments had an adverse effect on the net interest margin, but the fact that management had earlier decided to maintain a significant amount of interest-sensitive investments during this interval largely offset the negative impact. In summary, if retail loans and Reg Q deposits dominate the overall asset and liability system, a highly positive interest rate sensitivity position should probably be maintained at all times for defensive reasons.[9] As will be discussed in subse-

9. It has also been argued that the sensitivity of a major asset rate, the prime, tends to be less volatile than liability rates in the form of large CDs and borrowings. This would also suggest maintaining a positive position. Baker, "System Method," p. 124.

quent chapters, this policy decision will inevitably influence the management of the maturity structure of the government portfolio, and perhaps of the municipal portfolio, by requiring a greater short-term maturity position than might otherwise seem desirable.

In other words, discretionary funds management policies and tactics, including management of the investment portfolios, might logically operate under severe constraints because the normative asset and liability *system* prevailing in a bank makes the net interest margin vulnerable to a significant increase in interest rates and relatively invulnerable to a decrease in rates.[10] On the other hand, if the system match consists largely of floating rate loans against demand deposits and purchased funds, then defensive interest-sensitivity management is less imperative, and broader discretion regarding funds management policies becomes appropriate.

Interest-sensitivity management: positive

The objective here is to increase net interest margins through discretionary decisions to vary the relationship between interest-sensitive assets and corresponding liabilities based on a forecast of future interest rate probabilities. The implementation tactics would be to shorten asset maturities and lengthen liability maturities when rates are expected to rise and the converse when rates are expected to fall. Several constraints, however, tend to inhibit management in this area. First, events outside the effective control of management can materially affect the sensitivity position, thereby either making the risks of active management excessive or making the ex post results different from the ex ante objectives. For example, in the case cited in Table 4-2, even though management may have desired to enter 1979 with a significant positive sensitivity position, disintermediation of Reg Q-limited deposits and strong demand in retail loan programs may well have resulted in a positive sensitivity position below desired levels, despite reasonable efforts to maintain a short position in the investment portfolio.[11]

Second, the structure and behavior of yield curves may make the costs of active sensitivity management excessive. When rates are high and the con-

---

10. If firmly implemented in the future, the policy change of the Federal Reserve in October of 1979 to focus on the monetary base rather than the Fed Funds rate in executing monetary policy would reinforce this conclusion because it means that the possible range and volatility of short-term interest rates may be greater in the future than in the past.

11. Even in the wholesale commercial loan sector, outside pressures may frustrate active interest-sensitivity management. In 1976–77, when interest rates and loan demand had declined from their previous peaks (1974–75), large wholesale banks in response to competitive pressures from foreign banks were known to entice important borrowers by offering fixed rates on term loans. The result was to reduce the interest-sensitivity of the loan portfolio, even though funds management tactics may have concluded that increasing sensitivity would be desirable in view of the outlook for the next year or so.

sensus forecast is for a subsequent decline, it is typical for yield curves to be inverted; that is, short-term rates will be above intermediate- and long-term rates. Assuming a forecast predicting rate declines, active sensitivity management would dictate increasing short-term liabilities in order to fund somewhat longer asset maturities. Under inverted yield curve conditions, the spread at the time of such commitments could well be negative; if a general rate decline is delayed beyond expectations, the losses from carrying the negative spread could largely offset the returns derived from the operation.[12]

Similarly, when rates are low and expected to rise, yield curves have an upward shape; again, negative spreads prevail between the short assets and the longer liabilities that would be desired under active sensitivity management at such times. In brief, to increase the average net interest margin through active sensitivity management requires a correct forecast of both the direction and the extent of future interest rate movements and also, within reasonable limits, the timing of the changes.

Given the uncertainties and past forecasting records, a conservative policy toward positive interest-sensitivity management would seem desirable for most banks. This is not to say that policies should be entirely defensive, but that strict limits on the exposure should be improved. As shown in Table 4-3, only seven of the respondents indicated a completely defensive position on this score, but most indicated policy limits on exposures.

Interest sensitivity: appraisal techniques

Appraising the interest-sensitivity position of a bank at a given time has two dimensions: (1) establishing one or more time horizons and then accumulating the amounts of assets and liabilities that will be repriced at current interest rate levels during the specified time intervals, and (2) developing one or more techniques for integrating and monitoring the results derived from the accumulations. Table 4-3 shows the policies of respondent banks regarding these dimensions. Although a few indicated that a formal appraisal and monitoring system had not yet been adopted, the great majority regularly computed both the ratio of interest-sensitive assets (ISA) to interest-sensitive liabilities (ISL) and the absolute amount of the difference. A slight preference for monitoring via the absolute difference method rather than the ratio was indicated. The drawback to the ratio technique, particularly if used alone, is that a high or low ratio can be of minor significance if the absolute amounts of both the numerator (ISA) and denomi-

12. Merely lengthening the existing maturities of the investment portfolio, assuming no change in the liability structure, would not involve a negative carry cost, but the difference between short-term yields and long-term yields would represent an opportunity cost that may be excessive unless rates decline quickly.

TABLE 4-3

Interest-Sensitivity Appraisal Policies
(Respondent Banks: by Asset Size)

	Amount of Assets (in Millions of Dollars)					
	To 300		300–1,000		Over 1,000	
	Yes	No	Yes	No	Yes	No
Monitor Techniques:						
Ratio of ISA/ISL	10	2	10	2	5	3
Amount of ISA/ISL	11	1	11	1	8	—
Do not monitor		1		1		1
Time Horizon of Appraisal:						
1 month	6	2	2	10	2	6
3 months	8	0	3	9	2	6
6 months	6	1	2	10	1	7
1 year	5	3	11	1	7	1
None specified		4	—		—	
Active Management of						
Position:	10	3	9	4	9	—

nator (ISL) are small in relation to total assets and liabilities.[13] The ratio, however, does provide an indication of the relative effect of a change in interest rates; a positive ratio of 2 to 1, for example, indicates that a given change in rates will impact interest income twice as much as interest costs.

The amount of net ISA (ISA − ILS, which can be positive or negative) can give two valuable indications. First, it can be an indication of the change in net interest income that would result from a given change in interest rates, assuming that the change impacts asset yields and liability costs to about the same degree and that the net interest-sensitive amount remains constant. The relationship may be expressed as follows:

$$\triangle IR(ISA - ISL) = \triangle NII$$

13. For example, a bank with $500 million in assets that had $5 million in interest-sensitive assets and $1 million in interest-sensitive liabilities would show a positive interest-sensitivity ratio of 5, which would suggest that an increase in interest rates would materially improve earnings of the bank. But the small absolute difference of $4 million compared to the total size of the bank indicates that the effect would be minimal. It is doubtful if these proportions could actually be found in a bank of that size, but the point is that comparative ratio analysis alone may result in an erroneous conclusion.

where

$$\triangle IR \;=\; \text{change in average interest rates during period,}$$
$$ISA \;=\; \text{interest-sensitive assets,}$$
$$ISL \;=\; \text{interest-sensitive liabilities, and}$$
$$\triangle NII \;=\; \text{change in net interest income.}$$

For example, if interest rates increase by 100 basis points and ISA exceeds ISL by $50 million, then (other factors remaining constant) net interest income should increase by $500,000. The effect on the net interest margin can be computed by dividing this amount by total earning assets.[14]

Second, assuming ISA is positive, the amount of net ISA should give a rough indication of the disintermediation costs (Reg Q deposits into interest-sensitive liabilities) that can be tolerated before the net interest margin is subject to serious erosion. Disintermediation is, of course, a phenomenon associated with rising rates. As interest costs rise due to both higher rates and higher amounts of ISL, the cost increase can be offset by the increase in net interest income derived from the original excess of ISA over ISL. For example, if the positive net ISA position is $50 million and rates subsequently move up by 100 basis points, then $500,000 of the consequent disintermediation costs can be absorbed without significant impact on the net interest margin.

Interest sensitivity: time horizon

Because the planning period for most banks is on an annual basis, the general preference for a one-year time horizon as shown in Table 4–3 is not surprising. However, policies on this point varied widely; some banks used multiple horizons up to a year or more, some used one year only, and some limited the horizon to three or six months.

The argument for measuring the sensitivity position over a relatively short period of time has been expressed as follows:

> The literature on the subject suggests that a rate-sensitive asset or liability is any asset or liability that can be repriced within one year. Such a definition leaves much to be desired, inasmuch as interest rates on Fed Funds and the prime rate changed 200 to 300 basis points on several occasions within ninety days during the 1973–75 period. . . . The system method suggests that a ninety-day measure be used to define rate sensitivity because of experience during the 1973–75 period of rapidly changing rates.[15]

---

14. Note that a negative change (decline) in interest rates improves net interest income if the net amount of ISA is negative or, in other words, if ISL exceeds ISA.

15. Baker, "System Method," p. 124.

The change in monetary policy tactics toward direct management of the amount of bank reserves rather than to management of short-term interest rates (Fed Funds rates in particular) reinforces this conclusion. Presumably, if the new policy is firmly implemented, the Fed will tolerate considerably more volatility in short-term rates than formerly, although empirical experience over the next several years will be required in order to assess the actual effects of the policy change. As of the end of 1979, however, given the probability that short-term interest rates will be more volatile in the future than in the past, the most appropriate time horizons for sensitivity measurement would seem to be three and six months. Because respondents' indications of their time horizon preferences were obtained prior to the change in Federal Reserve policy, it would seem highly probable that the replies on this issue may not reflect their future policies.

It is doubtful, however, if the one-year time horizon will be abandoned completely, because profit plans and strategies to accomplish the profit plan objectives are based on annual projections of balance sheet and income statement items. Therefore, the one-year time horizon for interest-sensitivity appraisal would also seem appropriate. The profit plan projections of average amounts for various loan programs and various categories of core deposits should indicate probable changes in the sensitivity position. As the existing position is already known, the decision can be made as to whether, in the light of net interest margin targets and the outlook for interest rates, discretionary action to change the position is required.

As a consequence, a policy of using multiple time horizons may be recommended. Table 4–4 presents a hypothetical interest-sensitivity position based on three-month, six-month, and one-year horizons. In this example, the results show a significant decline in the positive sensitivity position between three and six months which may have been typical as of mid-1979, when the rapid growth in six-month money market certificates had the natural effect of loading liability sensitivity in the three- to six-month range. Based on this analysis, some moderate reallocation of the government portfolio from the six-month to one-year maturities to the less-than-six-month range might have seemed appropriate, particularly if bank management concluded that the outlook favored further pressure on interest rates through the last half of 1979.[16] In addition, pricing of loans on a floating rate basis might have been emphasized. The municipal six-month to one-year maturities might also have been screened for sale candidates, but any adjustments here would include tax and marketability considerations.

---

16. This illustration was written in July of 1979 so as to avoid hindsight resolve of interest rate levels. The fact that the new money market certificates replaced Reg Q-limited deposits on a significant scale at many banks in the first half of 1979 was a particular reason for monitoring the six-month sensitivity position at that time.

TABLE 4-4

Analysis of Interest-Sensitivity Positions:
Hypothetical Example
(as of June 30, 1979)

Interest-Sensitive Assets* (in Thousands)		Interest-Sensitive Liabilities (in Thousands)	
Fed Funds Sold	4,000	Repos, to 1 week	2,000
U.S. Governments:		Wholesale CDs:	
to 3 months	3,000	to 3 months	10,000
3-6 months	2,000	3-6 months	4,000
6 months-1 year	7,000	6 months-1 year	1,000
Municipals:		Money Market Certificates:	
to 3 months	2,000	to 3 months	10,000
3-6 months	3,000	3-6 months	15,000
6 months-1 year	5,000		
Commercial Loans:		Total	42,000
to 3 mos. (fixed rates)	5,000		
3 to 6 mos. (fixed rates)	3,000		
Floating rates	25,000		
Total	59,000		

Interest-Sensitivity Position:	Amounts		Net Amount	Ratios(ISA/ISL)
	Assets	Liabilities		
to 3 months	39,000	22,000	17,000	1.77
to 6 months	47,000	41,000	6,000	1.15
to 1 year	59,000	42,000	17,000	1.40

*Excludes amortization of installment and mortgage loans, which could be included if funds
are considered available for rollover into other instruments. See footnote 7 above.

Interest-sensitivity exposure

Although some portfolio decisions may be based on the existing interest-
sensitivity position, the interest-sensitivity exposure — based on *careful*
projections of the major loan and deposit categories — is of more importance
to funds management decisions.

As an illustration, assume that the data in Table 4-5 represent a six-
month projection of incremental fund requirements and sources based on
(1) inputs from the loan department, (2) an interest elasticity analysis of
Reg Q-limited deposits at expected interest rate levels and consequent estimated disintermediation of such deposits, and (3) prospective customer
demand for money market certificates. By combining the estimated fund

TABLE 4-5

Interest-Sensitivity Exposure Computation:
Hypothetical Example
(Six-Month Time Horizon)

	Amount	Legal Reserve Adjustment*	Net Required or Available
Fund Requirements:			
Loan increases:			
Fixed-rate	7,000,000	—	7,000,000
Floating rate	1,000,000	—	1,000,000
Deposit declines:			
Reg. Q-limited	8,000,000	.95	7,600,000
Total			15,600,000
Fund Sources:			
Deposit increases:			
Demand	2,000,000	.90	1,800,000
Money market certificates	18,000,000	.975	17,550,000
Total			19,350,000
Net Sources (sources less requirements)			3,750,000
Changes in Interest Sensitivity:			
Interest-sensitive assets:			
Loans			1,000,000
Liquidity increase (net sources)			3,750,000
Total increase in sensitive assets			4,750,000
Interest-sensitive liability increase:			
Money market certificates			18,000,000
Net increase in sensitive liabilities			13,250,000
Interest-Sensitivity Forecast:			
Interest-sensitive assets:			
Assets (existing position per Table 4-4)†			59,000,000
Increase (from estimation above)			3,750,000
Total			62,750,000
Interest-sensitive liabilities:			
Deposits and borrowing (existing position per Table 4-4)			42,000,000
Increase (from estimation above)			18,000,000
			60,000,000

(Continues)

Table 4-5 *(Continued)*

	Amount	Legal Reserve Adjustment*	Net Required or Available
Interest-sensitive position forecast			
Amount			2,750,000
Ratio			1.04

*This adjustment represents the amount of legal reserves that is released when a given deposit category declines or is required when a given deposit category increases. Percentages are estimated on the basis of legal reserve requirements as of 1979.

†Although the forecast position has a six-month time horizon, all assets and liabilities having existing maturities of more than six months but less than one year would have maturities of six months or less at the end of the forecast period. If the bank had interest-sensitive liabilities maturing between six months and one year (CDs), these would also become sensitive within a six-month time horizon at the end of the forecast period.

flow projections with the data in Table 4–4 showing the existing interest-sensitivity position, the estimated sensitivity position six months hence, or sensitivity exposure, can be calculated. The illustrative example shows only the forecasted position for a six-month time horizon, but of course forecasts for multiple time horizons might also be desirable in actual practice.

Note that the initial presumption is that all of the net sources derived from estimated deposit increases in excess of loan demand are applied to the acquisition of liquid assets, probably Fed Funds, until a further decision is made. Even so, the exposure analysis indicates that the existing six-month positive sensitivity ratio of 1.15 declines to a positive 1.04, assuming that the forecasted changes in the asset and liability sectors actually materialize. Given the probable error term in the forecasts, a reasonable interpretation of the exposure analysis is that expected events will probably result in a moderate deterioration of the interest-sensitivity position over the next six months. Therefore, the appropriate defensive tactics to implement this forecast would at the minimum require holding all deposit inflows in excess of those required to fund loan programs in short-term liquid assets. In addition, if management concludes that there is a high probability of further increases in interest rates, then moderate sales of investment portfolio assets with extended maturities (or, as a less likely alternative, purchases of CD funds with maturities of more than a year) might be made.

However, even assuming that management concludes that the probabilities favor a decline in rates over the next six months or so, an appraisal of probable changes in the asset and liability system outside of effective short-term control may still dictate holding net inflows in short-term assets or even increasing such assets for defensive reasons. For example, if increases in fixed-rate retail loans must be funded entirely or in part from wholesale CDs or money market certificates, then this sector will benefit significantly (improved net interest margin) from a decline in interest rates, which reduces funding costs while asset yields remain the same. Therefore, an appropriate defensive hedge against the opposite event (an increase in interest rates) would be to maintain or increase holdings of short-term investment assets. For example, if the mortgage portfolio based on outstanding commitments is expected to increase by (say) $5 million, then this can be regarded as an increase in the system investment in the long-term market which may inhibit lengthening of the investment portfolio despite a conclusion that the probabilities favor a decline in interest rates.

It should be expected that this hedge will incur some opportunity cost losses in the form of failure to tie down the current high rates with longer-dated portfolio assets; but given the great uncertainty of interest rate forecasts, the sacrifice may seem prudent. Lack of appropriate recognition of the hedging role of the discretionary investment portfolio as a means of controlling the desired interest-sensitivity exposure of the entire asset and liability system has been a major drawback to econometric models designed to optimize portfolio returns. The reason is that these models usually assume that maturity distributions of the investment portfolio can be structured independently of the entire system of assets and liabilities.[17]

Spread Management: Interest Arbitrage

Interest arbitrage options

For most banks of moderate size careful estimation, monitoring, and management of the interest-sensitivity position and estimated exposure may represent the entire spread management program. But interest arbitrage operations have also come to occupy a significant role in spread management programs in large banks. Interest arbitrage may be defined as the concurrent purchase and layoff of funds based on the estimated spread between the marginal cost of the funds and the marginal revenues on the assets acquired therewith. It may be presumed that most banks will oblige customers with respect to CDs and money market certificates on a reasonably competitive basis. Given that assumption, then in effect involuntary interest arbitrage operations may be forced on banks at times when the funds so acquired are not immediately needed to fund loan programs or declines in other deposit categories.

In addition, there may be an active policy to purchase significant

17. In an otherwise excellent book on econometric models and programs useful in managing bank investment portfolios, the policy constraints imposed on linear programming models designed to optimize portfolio returns do not explicitly include an interest-sensitivity position or exposure constraint. S. P. Bradley and D. B. Crane, *Management of Bank Portfolios* (New York: John Wiley and Sons, 1975), pp. 76–78 and pp. 117–20.

amounts of funds on a purely discretionary basis for arbitrage purposes. However, two observations concerning discretionary interest artibrage activities might be appropriate: (1) they do not represent intermediation as usually defined but are merely shifts of funds from one market sector to another, and (2) because spreads are very narrow, the result is to reduce the average net interest margin; but returns on capital may increase because interest arbitrage activities necessarily increase total leverage (assets-to-capital ratio), which may offset the decline in the net interest margin. The major categories of arbitrage activities are the following: (1) dealer spread operations in money market instruments, including Fed Funds, Eurocurrencies, and Treasury securities; (2) matched maturity arbitrage based on interest rate differentials between after-tax fund costs and after-tax yields on eligible assets; and (3) yield curve and interest rate forecast arbitrage on which asset maturities differ from liability maturities.

Most large banks have been market makers or dealers in money market instruments for many years. The operation requires making constant bid-ask quotations in the specified instruments; in theory, the spread profit is derived from the small dealer markup which exists on simultaneous trans-actions on both sides of the market. At any given time, however, discre-tionary long or short positions may be taken based on short-term forecasts (a hour to a few days) of the markets. Because of its nature, this activity is essentially a "trading operation," and it is conducted in a "trading room" where a quote board shows current yields on the relevant instruments. However, the dealer operation often provides a fairly constant source of funds to large banks, particularly in the Fed Funds market, because smaller banks typically maintain a Fed Funds sold position which is matched by the net Fed Funds purchased position of dealer banks. To the extent that this is true, the net purchases represent a source of funds for arbitrage into cate-gories (2) and (3).[18]

For illustrative purposes, Table 4–6 shows the yield and cost relation-ships prevailing in the money market in early March of 1979. Based on these data, matched maturity arbitrage might have been conducted in (1) Fed Funds purchased to broker call money where daily spread of 75 basis points existed or (2) money market certificates of six months (about 9.76 percent break-even yield as shown in Table 4–7) to six-month Eurodollar CDs of 11.20 percent or to six-month municipal notes where the tax equiv-alent yield at a tax rate of 48 percent was 10.19 percent.

Yield curve arbitrage was possible only by borrowing funds on a one-day

18. In a personal conversation with one banker in charge of funds management at a large bank with dealer operations, the comment was made that experience had shown a high degree of reliability of Fed Funds purchases from correspondent banks even during active restraint periods. Because the relationships here had been constant and close over long periods of time, a basic amount of net borrowings in the Fed Funds market was con-sidered more reliable than funds derived from the CD market.

TABLE 4-6

Asset Yields and Liability Costs
(Selected Instruments; as of March 1979)

	1 day	1 mo.	2 mos.	3 mos.	4 mos.	5 mos.	6 mos.	1 yr.
Asset Instruments:								
Fed Funds	10-10½	—	—	—	—	—	—	—
Call money	10¾-11¼	—	—	—	—	—	—	—
Commercial								
paper	—	9.85	10.00	10.10	—	—	—	—
Bankers								
acceptances	—	9.85	9.90	10.00	10.15	10.20	10.20	—
Eurodollar CDs	—	9.80	10.25	10.68	10.88	11.00	11.20	—
Treasuries &								
agencies	—	—	—	9.45	—	—	9.50	10.15
Municipal notes	—	—	—	—	—	—	5.30	5.30
Liability Instruments:								
Fed Funds	10-10½	—	—	—	—	—	—	—
Certificates of								
deposit*	—	9.75	10.00	10.20	NA	NA	10.70	10.30
Money market								
certificates	—	—	—	—	—	—	9.50	—

*Top rates paid by major banks; customer placements probably at lower rates.

TABLE 4-7

Break-Even Yields for Certificates of Deposit*
(Adjusted for Reserve Requirements and FDIC Expense)

	Break-Even Yields	
Rate Paid	Large CDs	Money Market Certificates
9.00	9.57	9.25
9.25	9.84	9.51
9.50	10.10	9.76
9.75	10.37	10.01
10.00	10.64	10.28
10.25	10.90	10.53
10.50	11.17	10.79
10.75	11.43	11.05

*Reserve requirements of 6 percent on CDs under 180 days and 2½ percent on money market certificates as of 3/1/79.

(Fed Funds) or one-month (CD) basis and incurring a maturity gap of at least three months via purchase of four- to six-month Eurodollar CDs. The risk in this operation was, of course, that short rates would continue to increase and, as a consequence, that the average funding cost during the maturity gap period would exceed the 10.88 to 11.20 percent derived on the four- to six-month Eurodollars. On the other hand, if rates declined during the gap interval, returns might be significantly increased; indeed, a strong belief that such a decline was likely could lead to a decision to assume an immediate negative spread position on grounds that the average cost of short-term funds during the gap interval would be less than the yield on the asset.

However, the major change in monetary policy implementation tactics in late 1979 may well result in a significant increase in the risks of yield curve arbitrage because short-term rates presumably will be considerably more volatile following the decision to abandon management of the Fed Funds rate as the operative tactical procedure. The following comment on the probable significance of the change seems very pertinent:

> The decision to eliminate a narrow Federal Funds rate target has introduced a substantial element of uncertainty, that should slow arbitraging in the credit markets. No longer can institutional lenders rely on that benchmark in estimating the spread relationships between the cost of their liabilities and rate of return on their assets.[19]

Therefore, although the long-term impact of the change in Fed tactics cannot be assessed, the logical near-term consequences probably will be significant revisions in policies with respect to yield curve arbitrage, so as to limit risk exposure. In particular, the rates on Fed Funds and other short-term borrowings may fluctuate by several hundred basis points from week to week so that it may be very difficult to predict average costs of such funds even over a time horizon of a few weeks. Thus, arbitraging daily funds into assets with maturities of only a few weeks may involve considerable risk.

During easy money periods, when the yield curve is upward-sloping, positive returns through arbitraging short liabilities into somewhat longer assets presumably might still be available. However, the opportunities have been rather limited in recent periods of relatively low interest rates. By way of example, the average and range of yields during 1977 on selected asset and liability instruments are shown in Table 4-8. Given these yield relationships, arbitrage of Fed Funds and one-month CDs into three- to six-month Eurodollar CDs would have been reasonably profitable on average during that year.[20] However, domestic asset instruments did not provide

---

19. H. Kaufman, *Comments on Credit* (New York: Salomon Brothers, Oct. 12, 1979), pp. 1–2.

20. The reasons Eurodollar CDs offer premium rates over domestic instruments have been subject to much debate. They include (1) absence of reserve requirements, (2) a more

TABLE 4-8

Averages and Ranges of Yields
(Selected Instruments, 1977)

	Maturities			
	1 day	1 month	3 months	6 months
Liability Cost (%):				
Fed Funds	5.4 (4.6–6.6)	—	—	—
CDs*	—	5.3 (4.6–6.4)	5.6 (4.7–6.7)	5.9 (4.8–7.1)
Eurodollar CDs	NA	5.6 (4.9–7.1)	5.9 (5.0–7.2)	6.2 (5.3–7.4)
Asset Yields (%):				
T-bills	—	5.0 (4.1–6.1)	5.2 (4.3–6.2)	5.4 (4.5–6.4)
Agencies	—	5.1 (4.2–6.3	5.4 (4.5–6.6)	5.7 (4.8–7.0)
Commercial paper	—	5.3 (4.5–6.4)	5.5 (4.6–6.6)	5.6 (4.7–6.7)
Eurodollar CDs	NA same as shown for liability cost			

*Effective costs after reserve requirements and FDIC costs estimated as follows: 1 month = 5.6, 3 month = 6.0, 6 month = 6.3.

any significant positive spreads over fund costs throughout the six-month maturity range.

The risk on the above arbitrage example was that the average cost of the Fed Funds purchased during the three- to six-month period would exceed the yield on the asset. And, of course, the upsloping yield curve during that year represented a consensus forecast of higher future interest rates. The estimated degree of risk on an arbitrage portfolio thus is a function of the following factors: (1) the amount of the original spread, (2) an assessment

competitive market, (3) larger average unit size and consequent economies of scale, and (4) a perceived risk that the country of domicile could block their availability. An excellent analysis of these reasons concludes that yield spreads are excessive between domestic and Eurodollar CDs, with the result that arbitrage opportunities become available because of market inefficiency. G. Dufey and I. H. Giddy, "The Unique Risks of Eurodollars," *Journal of Commercial Bank Lending*, June 1978, pp. 50–61.

of the outlook for average interest rates on the purchased funds over the period, and (3) the time difference between the asset and liability maturities, or maturity gap. If the gap is zero (assets and liabilities have matched maturities), then the risk in turn becomes zero, assuming negligible credit risk on the asset.

Clearly, if an active interest arbitrage operation is conducted, an information system to show the average existing spread and the gap position becomes desirable. A simple computer program can be designed to give the information on a daily basis. In practice, the assets and liabilities in an arbitrage portfolio would probably have daily maturities out to six months or more. The computer printout would list the maturities for each day separately, followed by a calculation of the weighted average yields and costs and the resultant net interest margin plus the average gap on the respective maturities.

To illustrate the concept, a simplified example might suffice. Assume that an arbitrage portfolio consists of three maturities of assets and liabilities as shown in Table 4–9. From the table, we determine that the gap period averages fourteen days and the net interest margin is .68 percent. In

TABLE 4–9

Maturity Gap and Yield Spread Analysis
(Arbitrage Position; Hypothetical Example)

Asset			Liability		
Amount	Maturity	Yield	Amount	Maturity	Cost
5,000,000	10 days	7.0%	10,000,000	1 day	6.0%
10,000,000	30 days	7.3%	10,000,000	30 days	7.0%
10,000,000	60 days	7.5%	5,000,000	60 days	7.2%
25,000,000			25,000,000		
Wt. avg. maturity 38 days			Wt. avg. maturity 24 days		
Wt. avg. yield 7.32%			Wt. avg. cost 6.64%		

this case, the gap could be largely closed by converting $5 million in one-day Fed Funds to sixty-day CDs. A decision might be made to close the gap either partially or entirely if the forecasted outlook for the average cost of Fed Funds over the next sixty days exceeded the current cost of sixty-day CDs.[21] Given an information system along the above lines, the risk on an arbitrage operation can be monitored daily and controlled accordingly.

21. Perhaps the most aggressive interest arbitrage transaction would be to assume a current negative spread position based on a forecast of declining interest rates over the gap period. Fed Funds at 11 percent converted to a six-month asset at 10.5 percent on the

Interest arbitrage policies: respondent banks

Table 4-10 shows the policies of the respondent banks with respect to the various arbitrage options discussed above.[22] As might be expected, large banks were more active in this area than those of moderate size. But while more than half of the banks with assets between $300 million and $1 billion had a completely negative policy toward this phase of spread management, a majority of the smallest group maintained that they had conducted

TABLE 4-10

Interest Arbitrage Policies
(Respondent Banks; by Size Groups)

| | Amount of Assets (in Millions of Dollars) | | | | | |
| | To 300 | | 300–1,000 | | Over 1,000 | |
	Yes	No	Yes	No	Yes	No
Matched Maturities:						
CDs	8	5	6	7	6	3
Borrowings	4	9	4	9	4	5
Asset Maturities Exceed Liability Maturities:						
CDs	5	8	4	9	6	3
Borrowings	6	8	3	10	7	2
Asset Maturities Less than Liability Maturities:						
CDs	5	8	4	9	3	6
Borrowings	5	9	3	10	1	8
Domestic Liabilities to Eurodollar Assets:	0	13	2	11	8	1

matched maturity spreads on large CDs. The following comment of one respondent typified the negative view toward interest arbitrage operations:

> Senior management does not agree with this approach. I concur also as cost of staff, space, etc., to perform functions may not result in (adequate) profit or control. At present we will pass.

---

basis of a forecast that Fed Fund rates will average less than 10.5 percent over the next six months would be an example. As noted above, given the change in Federal Reserve policy in late 1979, it is doubtful if current policies will permit such operations to any material extent.

22. Large respondents were requested to omit any dealer options in order to make the responses comparable for all banks.

References were also made to capital constraints and to lack of qualified managerial talent.

On the other side, a few noted that at certain times the need to maintain customer relationships required the purchase of large customer CDs when liquidity needs were minimal.[23] These banks noted that under these circumstances they were forced into an involuntary interest arbitrage operation despite their generally negative posture in this connection. In this case a definite preference for matched maturities was indicated, although a number of respondents indicated that moderate interest rate gap positions were acceptable.

In the case of larger banks, the great majority had a policy that permitted the assumption of an interest rate gap position. Both CDs and borrowings (largely Fed Funds) were normally acquired and spread into assets with longer maturities consequent to the typically upsloping nature of the yield curve.[24] However, a majority of these banks reported a negative policy toward arbitraging longer-dated CDs (say, three to six months) into shorter term assets. The negative responses in this connection can be construed as indicating that highly aggressive arbitrage operations were not part of normative policies. Presumably, these would sometimes include the acquisition of short-dated assets with longer-dated liabilities even at an existing negative spread based on a forecast of increased interest rates and a consequent projected average positive spread during the gap period. In addition, when the yield curve is inverted and there is a positive spread between long liabilities and short assets, market conditions often make it difficult to place CDs with extended maturities.

Finally, the responses showed clearly that the Eurodollar market remains almost entirely with the province of the large banks. In the past few years, for reasons discussed above, the most profitable arbitrage opportunities have been from domestic borrowings and CDs into Eurodollar CDs of foreign banks or foreign branches of domestic banks. All but one of the large banks indicated that they have used this market regularly in their spread management operations. But only two out of the twenty-six respondent banks with less than $1 billion in assets would consider the acquisition of Eurodollar assets. This is understandable in the case of banks with less than $300 million in assets, because the minimum unit of transaction is normally at least $1 million and preferably $3 million to $5 million. Therefore, participation in this market might require an excessive proportion of total assets. For banks with assets between $300 million and $1 billion,

23. Strong core deposit growth in excess of loan demand produces this condition. At such times, banks avoiding active interest arbitrage may desire to use the excess liquidity to lower the amount of large CDs outstanding.

24. Again, it should be noted that the responses referred to policies in effect prior to October of 1979. It is entirely possible that policies have changed considerably due to the structural changes introduced into the financial markets in that month.

however, the preponderance of negative responses suggests that their arbitrage policies are not entirely efficient, because the effect is to eliminate asset commitments in the market that has provided the most advantageous spread opportunities in recent years. Lack of familiarity with the nature of the market and the perception that offshore dollar assets may somehow constitute a greater risk even if they represent liabilities of highly reputable banks may be responsible for the negative policy posture; as Dufey and Giddy have shown, however, this latter risk appears negligible.[25]

25. Dufey and Giddy, pp. 53–57.

5

THE INVESTMENT PORTFOLIO:
GOVERNMENTS AND AGENCIES

The distribution of the investment portfolios of insured commercial banks at the end of 1964 and 1974 and at mid-1978 is shown in Table 5-1. Although these data show that the percentage of governments and agencies in the total security portfolio have significantly increased in the past several years, the relative role of these securities was still significantly less than in

TABLE 5-1

Distribution of Investment Portfolios
(Insured Commercial Banks; in Billions of Dollars)

	12/31/64		12/31/74		6/30/78	
	Amount	% of Total	Amount	% of Total	Amount	% of Total
U.S. Treasuries	$62.5	62.1%	$51.6	27.8%	$97.0	37.5%
U.S. Agencies*	—	—	31.0	16.7	39.5	15.2
Municipal Obligations	33.3	33.0	96.7	52.2	117.0	45.1
Other Securities	5.0	4.9	6.2	3.3	5.8	2.2
Total	$100.8	100.0%	$185.4	100.0%	$259.3	100.0%

Source: Federal Reserve bulletins.

*Agencies were not reported separately in 1964.

previous decades. Until the mid-sixties, these securities averaged about 65 percent of the total portfolio, but a steady decline ensued until the nadir was reached at year-end 1974, as shown in Table 5-1.

Governments: Portfolio Role

Government and agency securities have several properties which in theory should make them attractive for bank portfolios. These are as follows:

1. The regulatory authorities classify them as riskless assets for purposes of evaluating capital adequacy.
2. Maturity options are very extensive; weekly maturities are available for periods up to nine months and often several maturities for each year are available up to fifteen years or more.
3. They have excellent marketability properties; relatively large amounts can be purchased and sold at quoted prices through an extensive market system. Indeed, the Federal Reserve is committed to maintaining "orderly" market conditions in these securities.
4. They are universally acceptable for meeting pledging requirements on certain types of public deposits.
5. If a bank is a member of the Federal Reserve System, borrowing at the discount window is normally secured by governments.
6. Repos and reverse repos are customarily executed with these securities.

When demand deposits dominated the liability structure and liquidity needs were met from asset secondary reserves, the properties of short-term governments made them highly desirable for liquidity purposes. But with the advent of liability management (purchased funds) to cover liquidity requirements, the perceived need for secondary reserve assets has declined. Moreover, as a larger proportion of bank liabilities have become interest-bearing in nature and rates paid thereon have escalated, pressure on net interest margins has become chronic in the banking industry. The rational response to the cost pressure has been liquidation of governments because municipals typically offer significantly higher tax equivalent yields in the intermediate and long-term maturity sectors, and yield improvement in the short-term sector can be achieved through other types of money market assets (although at some moderate sacrifice in quality and marketability).

As a result, by year-end 1974 holdings of government and agency securities had declined to the smallest percentage of bank assets since before the Great Depression of the thirties.[1] But problems that surfaced during the "money crunch" of 1974 and the subsequent severe economic recession resulted in a reversal of this long-sustained trend in funds management policies. The first problem, alluded to in Chapter 3, was that market constraints on the availability and cost of purchased funds produced limits to their use as a liquidity source at the very time liquidity pressures were most intense. This led to public expressions of regulatory concern of which the following statement is an example:

---

1. Although for obvious public relations reasons bank investment officers are reluctant to be quoted publicly on the subject, the author has participated in private debates with these officers devoted to the premise that the only functional role of government and agency securities in a bank portfolio was that of covering estimated pledging requirements, assuming a risk asset-to-capital constraint was not operative in the bank.

Recent experience has demonstrated...what banking prudence itself should have dictated; namely, that the funds on which liability management depends can be quite volatile, especially if the maturities are short, and that banks may therefore have to wrestle with uncomfortable — even though they be temporary — liquidity problems.[2]

Unfortunately the problems of a few large banks and/or holding companies proved to be more than temporary, and their failure or forced merger received wide attention in the media.[3] The result was that a conservative image again became fashionable, as contrasted to the previously desired image of maximum growth through aggressive and innovative management. Because government and agency securities are considered both liquid and riskless, implementation of the new image would naturally include upgrading their role in the portfolio, despite the fact that after-tax yields on these assets have typically been less than the yields available on alternative obligations.[4]

Given this brief historical background, the major policy issues with respect to the government security portfolio might be summarized as follows: (1) the policies of banks, if any, with respect to the normative (minimum) size of this sector and the items considered eligible for inclusion; (2) the perceived functional role or roles of government securities in asset management policies; (3) policies with respect to the maturity configuration of the account; (4) cyclical timing policies, if any, associated with the management of the portfolio; and (5) policies with respect to tax management trading.

Portfolio dimensions

Table 5-2 shows the general policy guidelines of the respondent banks with respect to their governmental portfolio. The majority specified a target size for the government portfolio, and the most frequent determinant of the target was a specified percentage of assets. The normative specification for the government portfolio was generally between 5 and 10 percent of assets.[5]

2. Arthur F. Burns (Chairman, Board of Governors of the Federal Reserve System), "Maintaining the Soundness of Our Banking System," *Monthly Review* (Federal Reserve Bank of New York), Nov. 1974, p. 265.

3. For example, "Are the Banks Overextended?," *Business Week,* Sept. 1974, pp. 52–56. In this article, the documentation of failures, erosion of liquidity and capital positions, and serious problems in certain loan areas (loans to real estate investment trusts) produced the impression of a serious malaise in the banking industry.

4. The policy to maintain governments and agencies at specified amounts solely in order to produce the desired image of conservatism is generally known as "window dressing" and respondent banks, as noted below, were requested to include this factor in their priority rankings of the functional role of these securities in the asset structure.

5. Perhaps because it is easy to cite, a 10 percent target of assets or deposits is often found in published articles offering suggestions for written investment policies. For example, see

TABLE 5-2

Policy Parameters of Government Security Portfolio:
Amount and Types
(Respondent Banks; by Size Groups)

| | Amount of Assets (in Millions of Dollars) | | | | | |
| | To 300 | | 300–1,000 | | Over 1,000 | |
Policy Issue	Yes	No	Yes	No	Yes	No
Target Amount Specified	11	2	6	7	6	3
Determination of Target	(11)		(6)		(6)	
Percent of assets	6		4		4	
Percent of deposits	2		1		2	
Percent of portfolio	2		—		—	
Others specified:						
Pledging needs	1		—		—	
Repro needs	—		1		—	
Agencies as Full Substitute for Treasuries	8	5	8	5	5	4
GNMA pass-throughs included	1	12	3	10	5	4
Use of Government Futures Market	0	13	1	12	2	7

However, a significant minority (34 percent) indicated that they did not have a specific goal for this sector of the portfolio; the majority of these were the intermediate-sized banks. In these banks, the proportion of assets devoted to governments is determined on an ad hoc basis from the estimated functional needs as described below; because after-tax returns are generally less on governments than on alternatives, the account is maintained at the minimum consistent with such needs.

Government agency obligations have typically offered a yield advantage over Treasuries for maturities of more than a year. The apparent reasons are that (1) some investors, foreign nationals in particular, exclude the agency universe and (2) the marketability of large units is less assured than on Treasuries. On the other hand, the regulatory agencies include agencies along with Treasuries as riskless assets for purposes of capital adequacy evaluation, and on published statements the totals of the two were often combined.

In the short-term maturity sector, the bond equivalent yield of discount

D. L. Hoffland, "A Model Bank Investment Policy," *Financial Analysts Journal,* May–June 1978, p. 65.

Treasury bills usually approximates yields on coupon agencies, but as maturities are extended the yield spreads tend to increase. Table 5-3 shows the yield spreads (in basis points) prevailing during the twelve months ending in March 1979. Because the spreads have varied over a considerable

TABLE 5-3

Prevailing Yield Spreads
(In Basis Points; March 1978–March 1979)

Maturity	Yield Spread: Agencies vs. Treasuries		
	Maximum	Average	Minimum
1 year	27	3	– 29
2 years	55	12	– 10
3 years	39	15	– 16
5 years	37	17	5
7 years	38	24	10
10 years	42	23	9

Source: Salomon Brothers, Bond Market Roundup, March 16, 1979, p. 2.

range, a target spread is usually required before agencies are substituted for Treasuries; twenty to thirty basis points would seem to be reasonable on this score. But assuming an appropriate yield advantage, a strong argument can be made that agencies should be full substitutes for governments because their risk properties are minimal and their marketability properties are only slightly less favorable than governments.

As yet, only the largest banks consider the GNMA pass-through securities eligible for inclusion in the portfolio. These securities enjoy the unconditional guarantee of the government and also typically offer a positive spread of ten to twenty basis points over other agencies. However, the disadvantage is that the principal and interest payments on the pooled mortgages are passed through monthly and voluntary prepayments are also included; the result is that their use complicates both portfolio accounting and maturity scheduling of the portfolio. Therefore, only large banks with computer capacity sufficient to handle the technical difficulties regularly consider these securities.

Finally, with only a few exceptions respondents avoided any operations in the futures markets. The exclusion suggests that this relatively new market is regarded as a short-term trading area that is not compatible with prudent funds management policies. However, because the sale of futures contracts with roughly the same maturities as existing holdings has the effect of reducing the market risk exposure, a strong argument can be made that such hedging operations are protective rather than aggressive in nature. As banks become more aware of the potentials of the futures markets, funds management policies may well be modified to include hedging transactions in the futures markets.[6]

Perceived functional roles

Assuming (1) that most liquidity requirements can be met from purchased funds and (2) that the capital position does not constrain asset allocations to risk assets, then the role of the government and agency portfolio in fund management operations logically becomes peripheral in nature. Under these conditions, optimal funds management policies should strive to minimize its size.

A minimization strategy can be associated with two of the hypothesized functional roles shown in Table 5-4, pledging requirements and window dressing. If pledging requirements dominate the perceived functional role, then it may be presumed that the government account will be held at the minimum consistent with legal collateral requirements for specified categories of public deposits. In this case, the actual and forecasted levels of public deposits requiring government securities as collateral become the operative control mechanism determining the allocation of assets to this sector. However, only five banks (14 percent of the respondent universe) indicated that pledging requirements dominated the functional role of governments, although another thirteen (37 percent) put pledging requirements second in their priority rankings. The intermediate- and smaller-sized banks in particular tended to rank pledging needs near the top in their assessment of the alternative functional roles of the government account. The probable reason is that public deposits tend to represent a larger percentage of the total in these banks and corporate deposits a smaller percentage than is typical for the largest banks.

The "window dressing" role is based on the perception that it would not be prudent for published statements of condition to show governments as a percentage of assets (deposits) significantly below that of comparable banks. The following discussion of the structuring of a linear programming model to produce optimal asset/liability management policies is illustrative of this point:

> Initially, the model did not include any constraints on the governments-to-assets ratio. When some early runs of the model were discussed with management, they expressed considerable uneasiness about the results. The model was indicating

---

6. The following comment, by Sherwin Kite of GNP Commodities, Inc., is suggestive of this trend: "Originally it was primarily the biggest commercial banks and government securities dealers who were using the futures market as a hedge against interest rate increases. Now...there is definitely a new interest by secondary institutions—regional banks, money market funds, and many other customers who are affected by interest rates." *Wall Street Journal,* March 26, 1979, p. 20.

TABLE 5-4

Government Security Portfolio:
Priority Rankings of Functional Roles
(Respondent Banks; by Size Groups)

Asset Size (In Millions of Dollars)	Secondary Reserves	Pledging	Limit Risk Assets	Window Dressing	Regulatory Requirements	Return Maximization
Priority 1:						
To 300*	12	1	—	—	—	—
300–1,000†	5	4	1	2	—	1
Over 1,000‡	6	—	—	1	—	2
Total	23	5	1	3	—	3
Priority 2:						
To 300	—	8	1	—	2	2
300–1,000	2	4	2	2	2	1
Over 1,000	3	1	—	—	1	4
Total	5	13	3	2	5	7
Priority 3:						
To 300	—	2	4	1	1	2
300–1,000	1	—	3	—	1	4
Over 1,000	—	2	3	—	—	1
Total	1	4	10	1	2	7
Priority 4:						
To 300	—	—	4	2	1	2
300–1,000	4	—	4	1	1	1
Over 1,000	—	4	2	1	—	—
Total	4	4	10	4	2	3
Priority 5:						
To 300	1	1	1	1	2	2
300–1,000	1	—	1	2	6	2
Over 1,000	—	—	2	2	2	1
Total	2	1	4	5	10	5
Priority 6:						
To 300	—	—	—	3	2	2
300–1,000	—	—	1	5	2	3
Over 1,000	—	—	—	2	3	1
Total	—	—	1	10	7	6

(Continues)

Table 5-4 *(Continued)*

Asset Size (In Millions of Dollars)	Secondary Reserves	Pledging	Limit Risk Assets	Window Dressing	Regulatory Requirements	Return Maximization
No Functional Role:						
To 300	—	1	3	6	5	3
300–1,000	—	—	1	1	1	1
Over 1,000	—	2	2	2	3	—
Total	—	3	6	9	9	4

*N = 13
†N = 13
‡N = 9

that the bank should switch large amounts of its investment securities out of governments and into municipals. While this type of switch seemed to be very profitable, it implied balance sheets for the bank with far lower ratios of governments to assets than other large commercial banks had at that time. . . . In particular, the possible reactions of corporate treasurers and of investors in the market for bank stocks were the basis for managements' worries. If the bank were to publish a balance sheet in which the ratio of governments to assets was far lower than in other major commercial banks, it was felt that corporate treasurers and investors might begin to view the bank as being unsound.[7]

Appropriate functional risk and liquidity constraints based on management's assessment of these needs had previously been incorporated into the model; nevertheless, the model was further refined to include a required minimum percentage of assets devoted to governments. Therefore, it is clear that under the terms of the final model, the government portfolio was to be minimized subject to a window dressing constraint. As of 1979, however, only a few banks indicated that this was the principal role of the government portfolio, and about 75 percent of the sample held that window dressing had a very low priority (5 or lower) in their assessment of the alternative functional roles of this account.[8]

Table 5–4 shows that the majority (66 percent) of the respondents believe that the primary role of the government portfolio is to provide secondary reserve assets. As might be expected, this function was particularly dominant in the smaller banks, where active liability management is less feasible because of limited access to purchased funds. But it was surprising to find that while two-thirds of the largest banks gave this function the highest priority, less than half the intermediate-sized group did so. The difference in

7. K. J. Cohen, "Dynamic Balance Sheet Management: A Management Science Approach," *Journal of Bank Research,* Winter 1972, p. 13.

8. Because the window dressing role requires the admission that factors other than optimal fund management policies may be operative, respondents may have been somewhat reluctant to be entirely candid in their responses as to the real importance of this role.

the role ascribed to pledging requirements was largely responsible for the result. Large banks apparently consider pledging needs to be of minimal importance. In the intermediate group, however, these needs are ranked almost equal to the secondary reserve role; in fact, more of these banks listed pledging needs in their first two priority rankings than listed secondary reserve requirements.

In banking theory, the government portfolio is often viewed as the vehicle through which banks can either voluntarily control their risk asset exposure or conform to regulatory risk asset-to-capital guidelines. However, in practice the respondents considered control of the risk asset position to be of only moderate importance in determining fund allocations to governments; about 60 percent ranked this role in the bottom three priority categories. And there was definite resistance to the view that regulatory assessment of the risk asset position would have a significant impact on funds management policies. About 72 percent of the banks indicated that regulatory evaluations had either no role or a minimal role (priorities 5 and 6) in their determination of fund allocations to the government portfolio.[9]

Finally, there is the possibility that in some banks tax shelters derived from other sources (such as leasing activities) may make governments more attractive than municipals strictly on an income basis. In addition, because of superior marketability features, the government portfolio may be regarded as the principal source of returns derived from cyclical timing strategies in the bond markets. The data in Table 5–4 suggest there are major differences within the banking industry on this score. Two-thirds of the larger banks ranked return maximization high (priority 1 or 2), probably because these banks tend to be active in cyclical trading and have also developed alternative tax shelter activities. But only 15 percent (four of twenty-six) of banks with assets of less than $1 billion gave this function a similar ranking, and half gave this function a very low ranking (5 or below).

To summarize, the principal role of the government and agency portfolio of most banks appears to be that of providing a source of secondary reserves. In moderate-sized banks an additional major role is their use to satisfy pledging requirements against certain types of public deposits. Beyond these two functions, wide differences in the perceived roles are apparent. Some consider the window dressing feature significant, while others hold that earnings maximization is important. Finally, although the use of the government portfolio as a means of controlling risk asset exposure was not

---

9. The direct effects of regulation on funds management policies may be relatively minimal given respondents' views on the functional role of the government portfolio in their banks. If policies were sensitive to regulatory evaluations, then it might be expected that control of risk asset exposure would be perceived as a major function of the government portfolio.

ignored, this role was decidedly of secondary importance in the opinion of most respondents.

Maturity Policies

Our hypothesis with respect to maturity policies was that most banks would be likely to have some normative maturity guidelines, but tactical flexibility to permit departure from norms would also be probable. Published data on the maturity distribution of the banking system's government portfolio are available, and the data for two selected dates are shown in Table 5-5. The first date, year-end 1976, represented a period of high

TABLE 5-5

U.S. Government Securities:
Holdings of Commercial Banks by Maturity*
(Selected Dates; in Billions of Dollars)

Maturity	Amount as of 12/31/76	Amount as of 6/30/79
Within 1 year	$31.2	$21.9
1 to 5 years	40.0	36.0
5 to 10 years	6.3	7.4
10 to 20 years	.3	1.1
Over 20 years	.4	1.4
Total	$78.1	$67.8

Source: Federal Reserve bulletin, Oct. 1979, p. A33.

*Data source reports that survey on holdings includes about 80 percent of systemic totals.

liquidity (low interest rates), while the second date, mid-1979, reflected monetary restraint and interest rates believed to be above normative levels. These data suggest the following dynamic behavioral characteristics of the government portfolio on a systemic basis:

1. Amounts committed to this sector tend to be subject to considerable variation as monetary conditions change; over the interval covered in Table 5-5, as monetary policy moved toward moderate restraint, bank holdings of governments declined by about 13 percent.
2. Maturities tend to be front-end-loaded; the largest proportion mature within one year and 85 to 90 percent within five years.
3. Maturity extension takes place on a moderate scale as interest rates rise, but even so the amounts committed for long periods (beyond ten years) tend to be relatively insignificant.

The first two characteristics are consistent with the secondary reserve role of the government portfolio. In implementing this role, total holdings of governments should decline as monetary restraint is imposed, and maturities should logically be front-end-loaded to minimize losses consequent to the required liquidation.

At this point it might be relevant to note that some academic research on optimal maturity strategies designed to produce efficient portfolios has failed to capture effectively the "accordion" property of the government account. Returns and risks (variability of returns) are usually compared on alternative portfolio maturity policy options, on the assumption that the total size of the account remains constant.[10] It is, of course, very difficult to simulate the probable dimensions of the accordion effect at various points in the interest rate cycle; nevertheless, its existence suggests that a front-end-loaded maturity structure may be more efficient, given the principal functional role of the portfolio.

The third characteristic supports the hypothesis that policies allow a moderate degree of tactical management of the maturity structure. The objective, of course, is to maximize total returns (and avoid losses) by lengthening maturities when interest rates are perceived to be high and shortening the structure when rates are perceived to be low.

The maturity policies of the respondent banks shown in Table 5-6 conform closely to the systemic characteristics. About 64 percent had a front-end-loaded maturity policy as compared to 28 percent that preferred a laddered structure and 6 percent that used the barbell approach. About 75 percent indicated maximum maturity limits of ten years or less; and, consistent with the front-end-loaded structure, about the same proportion indicated that the average maturity of the government portfolio was normally four years or less.

The nature of the typical yield curve structure in the government market would support a ten-year maturity limit. Table 5-7 shows the configuration of the yield curve during high and low interest rate periods for the past several years. Maturities beyond ten years provided an improvement of only twelve basis points even at the low point of the most recent interest rate cycle (the time when, in theory, extensions of maturity should receive their greatest reward). And during cyclical highs, extensions beyond ten years have offered lesser or even negative premiums.[11]

---

10. Cf. S. P. Bradley and D. B. Crane, "Simulation of Bank Portfolio Strategies: Laddered vs. Barbell Maturity Structure," *Journal of Bank Research,* Summer 1974, pp. 122–34; and G. H. Hempel and J. B. Yawitz, "Maximizing Bank Returns," *The Bankers Magazine,* Summer 1974, pp. 103–14.

11. When interest rates are low and are presumably expected to rise in the future, a preference for short maturities is to be expected which should be reflected in higher yield premiums offered on long maturities relative to shorter maturities. The opposite preference should be indicated at cyclical highs in rates because capital gains consequent to a subsequent decline in rates are greatest in the long sector and short maturities must be rolled over at lower rates.

TABLE 5-6

Maturity Policies for Government and Agency Portfolio
(Respondent Banks; by Size Groups)

	Amount of Assets (in Millions of Dollars)		
	To 300	300–1,000	Over 1,000
Maturity Structure:			
Laddered	3	3	4
Front-end loaded	10	9	4
Barbell	—	1	1
Maximum Maturity (Years):			
5 or less	3	1	4
5 to 10*	7	9	3
Over 10	1	—	1
No policy limits	2	3	1
Average Maturity (Years):			
1 to 2	—	2	—
2 to 3	4	5	4
3 to 4	6	3	—
4 to 5	2	2	4
5 to 10	—	1	—
Omitted	1	—	1

*A ten-year maximum was the modal response; fifteen of thirty-five (43 percent) gave ten years as their maximum maturity limit.

TABLE 5-7

Government Market: Yield Curve Structure (1974–79)

	Market Yields		
Maturity	1974 highs	1975–76 lows	Oct. 1979
3 months	9.86%	4.37%	13.04%
1 year	10.07	4.81	13.35
2 years	9.09	5.31	12.53
3 years	8.76	5.61	11.97
5 years	8.61	6.05	11.31
7 years	8.50	6.39	11.15
10 years	8.52	7.21	10.97
20 years	8.63	7.33	10.43
30 years	8.63	7.33	10.28

Source: Federal Reserve bulletins.

Maturity management

Respondents generally favored a policy of extending average maturities, but *not* the maximum maturity, during high interest rate periods. Presumably, the reason was to "lock in" the prevailing high yields and also to improve the amount of potential capital gains that would result from a subsequent decline in rates. However, the tactics employed to consummate maturity extensions suggest that highly aggressive maturity shifts are unusual. The responses in this connection are shown in Table 5–8. While a

TABLE 5-8

Maturity Management Tactics
(Respondent Banks; by Size Groups)

	Amount of Assets (in Millions of Dollars)		
Tactic	To 300	300–1,000	Over 1,000
Gradual and moderate changes	12	9	6
Large shifts at target rate level	1	4	3

greater proportion of the larger banks had followed aggressive tactics on maturity extensions during high interest rate periods (and presumably the converse when interest rate levels were low), the significant majority (even among banks with assets in excess of $1 billion) were inclined to use a moderate and gradualist approach. The well-known failure of forecasting models to predict the parameters of interest rate movements in the past several years was cited by some as the reason for their conservative posture toward cyclical maturity management.

This same lack of confidence in interest rate forecasting techniques may also be responsible for the distinct lack of popularity of the barbell maturity structure (used by only two banks). Under this structure, the normative portfolio consists of equal amounts of short maturities (one to three years) and longs (fifteen to twenty years), with little, if any, in between. The concept of management under this structure has been described as follows:

> Barbell portfolios tend to be trading portfolios, and it is typical for the long-term proportion of the portfolio to be largest when interest rates are high and for the short-term portion of the portfolio to grow when rates are low. Managerial expertise is clearly a prerequisite for the barbell maturity structure.[12]

Adoption of the system approach to asset-liability management may also inhibit cyclical maturity management. It was shown in Chapter 4 that as

12. G. H. Hempel and J. B. Yawitz, *Financial Management of Financial Institutions* (Englewood Cliffs, N.J.: Prentice-Hall, 1977), pp. 110–11.

interest rates move upward to high levels the liability system inevitably becomes more interest-sensitive: wholesale CDs, borrowings, or money market certificates replace Reg Q-limited deposits. In essence, this represents an involuntary shift of the liability system toward a much higher interest-sensitivity position. Unless positive action is taken to maintain or even increase asset sensitivity, a negative net sensitivity position beyond policy limits may result and, as a consequence, maturity extensions may well be precluded.[13]

Moreover, during high interest rate periods when the yield curve is inverted, yields derived from long maturities may be less than the marginal costs of purchased funds, including money market certificates. This condition resulted in the following comment from one respondent: "We decided to stay short in the government portfolio in late 1978 in order to avoid a negative carry on the marginal cost of funds." It can be argued, of course, that the negative carry should be temporary, assuming a subsequent cyclical decline in interest rates; but the uncertainties associated with the timing of the event might well inhibit major maturity extensions of the government portfolio.

Finally, the timing of cash flows to the investment portfolio usually inhibits active maturity management. In periods of low interest rates, loan demands are usually weak and inflows of core deposits strong. The result is that the investment portfolio receives maximum cash inflows during low points in the interest rate cycle. Rebuilding of the defensive liquidity position via an increase in secondary reserves and a reduction in the purchased funds position may mitigate the usage problem of the inflows to some extent, but even so significant amounts of additional funds are typically available for the investment portfolio. Appropriate cyclical maturity management would dictate placement of these funds in short maturities, but at these times short-maturity yields may be close to or less than rates on core time and savings deposits. To avoid negative spreads and to support earnings eroded by decreased loan demand, moderate extension of maturities may seem advisable, particularly since extension will result in significant relative yield improvement due to the sharp upsloping yield curve that typifies low interest rate periods.

13. The significant increase in six-month money market certificates (first authorized in June of 1978) in the last few months of 1978 and early 1979 took place after most respondents had returned their policy questionnaires. However, subsequent oral communication with some respondents generally supports this conclusion. Despite the availability of yields of 9.5 percent or higher on government and agency maturities of five years or so, a few reported even in mid-1979 that sales of intermediate maturities acquired a few months earlier had been made to keep the interest-sensitivity position at target levels. These targets generally were moderately positive, given the high inflation rate and consequent uncertainties as to whether further tightening of monetary policies would be forthcoming. In view of subsequent events in October of 1979, this conservative posture toward interest-sensitivity exposure was well rewarded late in the year.

Then, of course, when interest rates rise, intermediate and long maturity bonds show significant price declines, and cash flows to the investment portfolio may be reduced to zero or even become negative at the very time when yields are most attractive. In other words, liquidation of short maturities may be required to fund loan demand and thus cannot be used for maturity extension. And, as noted above, to acquire long maturities with purchased funds entails immediate negative spreads, even assuming that policy limits on purchased funds do not restrict their use for this purpose. Respondents were asked whether, given this typical behavior of cash flows, liquidity considerations have in fact constrained active maturity management during recent high interest rate periods. The responses are shown in Table 5-9. Intuitively, it might be expected that liquidity constraints would affect large banks to a greater degree than small banks because large banks have a higher proportion of their business in the volatile corporate banking markets where cyclical fluctuation in loan demand has usually been greatest. Indeed, both in 1969–70 and 1974–75, there was clearly a direct relationship between bank size and liquidity constraints on the maturity management of the investment portfolio.[14]

TABLE 5-9

Liquidity Constraints on Maturity Management
(Respondent Banks; by Size Groups)

Interest Rate Period	Management Constrained	
(Assets in Millions of Dollars)	Yes	No
1969–70:		
to 300	3	10
300 to 1,000*	8	4
over 1,000	9	—
1974–75:		
to 300	7	6
300 to 1,000*	10	2
over 1,000	8	1
1978 (to Nov.):		
to 300	9	4
300 to 1,000*	5	7
over 1,000	3	6

*One respondent in this size group did not answer question.

14. In 1969–70, the fact that Reg Q rate limits then applied to wholesale CDs as well as to retail saving and time deposits made that episode particularly painful for large banks because these wholesale funds thus became subject to very extensive disintermediation. The actual spread between Reg Q limits and market rates was, however, less than that in subsequent monetary restraint periods, which insulated retail deposits to some degree.

However, the 1978 episode represented an exception. Two reasons might be suggested: (1) corporate loan demand continued to be sluggish through 1978 but in contrast retail loan demand (installments, credit cards, and mortgages) increased rapidly; and (2) the introduction of money market certificates in mid-1978 subsequently intensified the disintermediation of Reg Q-limited deposits, and smaller banks have always had a larger portion of their total funds generated by Reg Q deposits. But although each interest rate cycle has had its unique characteristics, the overall evidence supports the proposition that maintenance of interest-sensitivity targets along with forced liquidation for liquidity requirements significantly inhibits active cyclical management of the government portfolio.

Tax management

As part of or in addition to active maturity management policies designed to increase returns through interest rate cycles, portfolio transactions based on tax considerations are often appropriate. In banks, realized capital losses are fully deductible from taxable income, so under existing law the net earnings effect of a capital loss is reduced by the factor: (1 – Marginal Tax Rate).

Although the exact timing of any tax savings represents a minor technical problem in evaluating the desirability of tax-oriented transactions, Table 5–10 shows an evaluation format of a hypothetical tax switch transaction.[15] The source of the return advantage is essentially the availability of the tax savings for investment into a replacement bond. The coupon on the replacement is assumed for illustrative purposes to be equal to the yield to maturity on the market price of the bond to be sold. Given this assumption, a total return advantage of about $35,000 is realized over the six-year period, and reported pretax income in future years will be about $11,600 higher than would be the case if the switch had not been made. Therefore, in addition to an increase in total returns over the entire maturity horizon, a moderate "built-in" improvement in future annual earnings is obtained at the sacrifice of a reduction in current reported earnings after security transactions.[16] Given the fact that the future outlook is always uncertain, this

---

15. Sale of a given bond at a loss and its immediate repurchase is prohibited under "wash" sale rules. Different issues, therefore, are required for sale and purchase, but in the government sector availability of numerous issues makes this requirement a trivial problem. Also, realized capital gains are fully taxable in the case of banks, and there is no "wash" sale rule on gains.

16. A technically more accurate evaluation of a tax management transaction would be to compute and compare the present value of the stream of coupons and the principal at maturity of the bonds to be sold and the bonds to be purchased. But, except in marginal cases, the conclusions as to desirability will not be changed, and the method used in Table 5–10 is more easily explained to the board of directors who usually must approve any transactions involving significant amounts.

TABLE 5-10

Tax Management Illustration: Evaluation of Effects

	Total Return Comparison	Per Year Comparison
Sale Data:		
Income @ 8% for 6 years	$480,000	$80,000
Capital loss:		
$1,000,000		
− 932,500		
$67,500		
Tax saving (48%) = $32,400	35,100	
Total opportunity cost of sale	$515,100	
Purchase Data:		
$965,000 @ 9.5% for 6 years	$550,650	$91,625
Total return advantage for 6 years	$34,950	
Income pickup for each year		$11,675

Note: Calculations are based on the following assumptions:
(1) Sale of $1,000,000, six-year, 8-percent coupon bond at a 9.5-percent yield-to-maturity basis (about $932,000); pretax loss of $67,500.
(2) Tax rate of 48 percent; after-tax loss of $35,000; tax saving of $32,400.
(3) Reinvestment of proceeds from sale ($932,500) plus tax saving ($32,400, rounded up $100 for computational ease) into a six-year, 9.5-percent coupon bond.
(4) The bank has a positive tax liability derived from other sources.

automatic contribution to the earnings growth path may be regarded as highly desirable.

However, there is the further implicit premise that management is willing to reduce current reported income in order to maximize total returns and generate higher future income. This behavioral problem has been well expressed as follows:

> The first consideration is how much of a reduction in reported net income the owners of the bank are willing to accept. Current accounting rules require that attention be focused on net income after securities' gains and losses rather than on net operating earnings. Explaining to stockholders that reductions in profits are advantageous is not easy.[17]

Operational tax management policies, therefore, may be constrained despite clear arithmetic return advantages. Of the respondent universe,

17. Hempel and Yawitz, *Financial Management,* p. 113. In publicly owned banks "Board of Directors" might be substituted for "owners" in the quotation.

nine (25 percent of the total universe of thirty-six) stated that they had a negative policy toward tax management operations. One offered the following comment: "We should take losses to improve future returns; however, the Board of Directors fails to comprehend the benefits of such a program." The negative posture, as might be expected, was concentrated almost entirely in the smaller size groups; only one bank with assets in excess of $1 billion reported an aversion to active tax management of the investment portfolio.

But even in banks with a positive policy toward tax management, the extent of tactical implementation will probably depend on a loss toleration evaluation. This would involve a comparison of expected operating earnings before discretionary tax losses with targeted earnings goals, and tax losses would be authorized to the extent that earnings goals would not be significantly impaired. For example, assuming an earnings growth rate target of 10 percent, the evaluation might be as follows:

Reported earnings, preceding year	$4,000,000
Expected earnings, current year[18]	$5,000,000
Target earnings (10 percent target growth rate)	$4,400,000
Maximum after-tax loss allowed	$600,000

To allow for a reasonable margin of error in the expected earnings results, the asset and liability committee and/or the board may authorize tax loss sales of $500,000 divided by the factor of $(1 - \text{tax rate})$. At the existing corporate tax rate of 48 percent, this action would limit tax management transactions to gross losses of about $960,000. In some instances, the loss authorization might be reduced because of discretionary losses taken in other asset sectors — the mortgage portfolio, for example, because of its lack of interest sensitivity. But given the structure of existing tax laws applicable to banks, there would seem to be strong reasons to include an annual tax management program as a specific element in fund management policies.[19]

18. Probably based on realized results through at least two quarters and preferably three quarters.

19. All assets that can be sold in the secondary markets should be included in the tax management program. These would normally include governments, municipals, and mortgages. However, the marketability properties of the individual items in these portfolios (with the exception of governments) may have to be reviewed in light of existing conditions in the financial markets.

6

THE INVESTMENT
PORTFOLIO: MUNICIPALS

The municipal portfolio has two components for which policy criteria are usually quite different. First, through competitive bidding or private negotiation, banks acquire the obligations of local governmental units. These units are existing or prospective deposit customers who may use other bank services, such as the trust department for pension fund management or data processing services. The second component consists of obligations purchased in the secondary market on an impersonal basis where the sole criterion for purchase (sale) is an objective evaluation of risk and return data related to the objectives and constraints of the asset and liability system prevailing within the bank.

The Municipal Portfolio: Local Obligations

Assuming a valued customer relationship with a municipal unit, the policy criteria for acquiring their obligations should closely resemble those used for customer loan accommodation. A typical example would be the short-term tax anticipation notes of a local municipal customer. These are usually sold on a competitive bid basis, and municipal finance officers have every reason to expect strong bids from their banks of account; the tax equivalent prime rate (Prime Rate $\times$ [1 – Tax Rate]) would be a normal pricing expectation with some variations depending on prevailing competitive conditions in the local banking markets. But the important point is that while technically these are classified as investment securities, functionally they are properly construed as customer loans.[1]

---

1. The Community Reinvestment Act passed by Congress in 1978 may result in even greater inducement to purchase local government obligations. Undr the terms of this statute banks are to be held accountable for credit flows to support the local community and presumably the evaluation would include evidence of willingness to extend credit to local municipal units.

The obligation to acquire local municipal debt is more ambiguous on serial and project bond issues underwritten by investment bankers; moderate participation would usually be considered expedient, but only if maturity and yield targets can be satisfied. Large banks might serve as principal underwriters or syndicate participants for these issues, in which case their portfolio acquisitions might depend on external market demand. If demand is weak, significant amounts may be acquired; but if demand is strong, then only residuals may be picked up, again assuming that yields and maturities are within policy limits.[2]

The data in Table 6-1 clearly support the proposition that local municipal obligations represent a unique sector of the investment portfolio. With-

TABLE 6-1

Policies on Local Municipal Issues*
(Respondent Banks; by Size Groups)

	Amount of Assets (in Millions of Dollars)					
	To 300		300–1,000		Over 1,000	
	Yes	No	Yes	No	Yes	No
Acquisition Policies:						
Actively bid	11	2	13	—	9	—
Rating required	3	10	—	13	1	8
Correspondent Participation on Bids:						
Often	—		2		1	
Sometimes	6		2		4	
Rarely	4		8		3	
Never	1		1		1	

*Defined as those municipal units having deposit accounts at the bank.

out exception, respondents with more than $300 million in assets had a firm policy of making strong competitive bids for local short-term debt issues, and only a small minority of the smallest banks indicated that their policy did not require such bids. Moreover, the strong consensus was that a formal credit rating was not an eligibility requirement for these obligations. In the absence of a rating the bank might be required to justify the credit to the

2. In a few publicized cases, notably Cleveland and New York, credit difficulties have caused considerable tension between local banks and municipal governments. But despite serious credit problems in these cities, the portfolios of the local banks had significant amounts of these debt obligations, suggesting that the notes and bonds were acquired on some basis other than a strictly impersonal investment evaluation.

regulatory authorities; but despite this drawback only a few banks required a rating for local issues.

Because legal loan limits do not apply to municipal general obligations, there is less reason to seek correspondent participation on large credits than on private sector loans. However, to relieve liquidity pressures, and perhaps for purposes of risk diversification or public relations, joint bids of two or more banks are sometimes submitted on short-term municipal borrowing. Still, the majority of respondents indicated that they used participation bids only infrequently. Even the largest banks reported only occasional requests for participation, despite their extensive correspondent networks. Under tight money conditions, liquidity considerations may increase the incidence of participation bids, but the general policy seems comparable to loan participation policy: invite participation only if it is clearly inappropriate for the major bank of account to handle the credit independently.

The Municipal Portfolio: Nonlocal Sector

Fund allocation policies

Assuming other intermediation programs generate a positive tax position, municipal bonds typically offer the most attractive after-tax returns of eligible alternatives in the secondary markets.[3] Therefore, the municipal portfolio has been an important source of income for most banks; particularly in larger banks, its size often significantly exceeds the government and agency portfolio.[4]

Between 1966 and 1978 member bank holdings of municipals (including locals) increased from about $34 billion to about $82 billion, which amounts to an average compound growth rate in excess of 7 percent. Compared to the loan portfolio,this rate of growth was only moderate, but it greatly exceeded that of the government portfolio. More important, during periods of cyclical liquidity pressures, aggregate bank holdings of municipal obligations have continued to increase, indicating that the municipal

3. An exception has been in the less than one year maturity sector during tight money periods when the yield curve becomes inverted on taxable securities but remains upsloping in the municipal market. For example, one-year prime municipals were quoted at a 5.10 percent yield at the end of March 1979, for a taxable equivalent yield of 9.81 percent at a 48 percent tax rate compared to a 10.60 percent yield on prime Eurodollar CDs. But beyond one-year maturities the taxable equivalent yield of prime municipals exceeded both Treasury and high-grade corporate yields. Salomon Brothers, *Bond Market Roundup*, March 30, 1979.

4. As of the end of 1978, U.S. Treasuries in the large weekly reporting banks amounted to $41.5 billion compared to the municipal obligation holding of $52.6 billion. As holdings of governments exceeded municipals in the entire banking system, smaller banks obviously had a relative preference for governments.

portfolio is not generally considered a source of liquidity and that spreads may be particularly attractive during such periods. For example, during the first half of 1974 (a period of severe monetary restraint), member bank holdings of governments declined by more than $4 billion (7 percent), while municipal holdings increased by $2.4 billion (3 percent).[5]

In funds management programs, therefore, it appears that the role of the municipal investment portfolio (exclusive of locals) is a combination of the following: (1) to provide the optimal outlet for that portion of the core deposits which is not required for liquidity and loan programs; (2) to provide maximum after-tax spreads on purchased funds; and (3) to provide an ultimate, although not normative, source of liquidity. If the first role is dominant, then the municipal portfolio logically becomes a "residual" in the funds management process modified for any tax or risk constraint considered appropriate. This means that a bank would project core deposit levels, then subtract estimated loan program needs, asset liquidity requirements, and technical needs for governments as discussed in the preceding chapter, and the balance would be available for municipals.

Table 6-2 indicates that the "residual" approach to the construction of the municipal portfolio dominates in banks with less than $1 billion in assets. However, a minority of these banks indicated that a target amount of risk assets in relation to capital was the prime determinant of fund allocation to municipals. In these instances, less than optimal returns on discretionary funds management programs would be realized, because capital adequacy

TABLE 6-2

Municipal Portfolio: Fund Allocation Policies
(Respondent Banks; by Size Groups)

| | Amount of Assets (in Millions of Dollars) | | | | | |
| | To 300 | | 300–1,000 | | Over 1,000 | |
	Yes	No	Yes	No	Yes	No
Allocation Policies:						
Profit (asset) plan used	13	—	13	—	6	3
"Residual" on profit plan	12	1	10	3	1	8
Allocation Constraints:						
Capital adequacy	1	12	3	10	4	5
Liquidity (interest sensitivity)	10	3	6	7	6	3

5. Federal Reserve bulletins, May 1974, p. A18, and March 1975, p. A18. Because local municipals are included in the data, the true investment portfolio may have remained relatively constant. In this section the municipal portfolio will be defined as holdings exclusive of locals.

problems would result in the substitution of lower-yielding, riskless assets for municipal investments.[6] Liquidity, including interest-sensitivity targets, represents the major reason why the "residual" is not fully allocated to municipals at certain times. If a strong probability of rising interest rates is perceived, then a position of high liquidity and positive interest sensitivity becomes desirable. Because the availability of municipals with maturities of six months or less is limited and yields are often unattractive even on a tax-adjusted basis, the municipal portfolio does not offer an optimal means of increasing the positive short-term interest-sensitivity position.

On the other hand, when interest rates are high and the perceived outlook is for a future decline, then a reduction in the positive interest-sensitivity position may be appropriate, and additional commitments to municipals in order to lock in the high rates become theoretically desirable. The problem here is that the sensitivity of the liability sector may have increased substantially due to significant increases in money market certificates and purchased funds and declines in Reg Q-limited deposits. As a consequence, major discretionary action to reduce the interest sensitivity of the asset structure may be inhibited; nevertheless, most respondents indicated an explicit policy of acquiring long-dated municipals during high interest rate periods, assuming the system position would tolerate such acquisitions.

The contrast between large banks and those of moderate size in the method used to determine fund allocations to the municipal portfolio was striking; large banks, with one exception, did not use the "residual" approach. There are two major differences in the nature of their operations which may account for the difference in approach. First, tax shelters from other sources, such as leasing and international activities, often reduce the need for tax-exempt income from municipals. In this case, the assumption made above — that there is net taxable income from other sources — may not be true, and tax planning thus becomes the determining factor in fund allocations to the municipal sector.[7]

Second, large banks are more inclined than small banks to conduct active spread management operations (interest arbitrage) with purchased funds. Municipals then become one of a set of alternative asset vehicles for match-

---

6. As noted in Chapter 2, the long-term remedy for funds management constraints imposed by inadequate capital would be to find appropriate means of improving the capital position. It would, of course, be desirable to compute the net result of additional capital on the return on equity. This involves balancing the higher net interest margin resulting from the substitution of municipals for riskless assets against the effect of the reduction in the capital leverage resulting from the addition of capital.

7. Taxable securities would be purchased until the projected taxable income becomes zero (or somewhat above zero if a policy to pay some income tax is adopted for public relations reasons), and only then would municipals be acquired with any additional funds available.

ing marginal yields with marginal costs of the purchased funds. If yields on municipals at given maturity targets offer a better yield spread than those available on alternatives (adjusted for taxes), then the factors constraining their acquisition become the tolerable maturity gaps and, in some cases, the perceived reliability of funds to maintain the spread position (liquidity) and/or the capital available to support the risk asset exposure. As expected, therefore, a greater proportion of large banks than of small banks reported capital adequacy and liquidity considerations as constraints on fund allocation to municipals.

Portfolio Configuration

Portfolio configuration: quality

Table 6-3 shows respondents' policies with respect to credit evaluations

TABLE 6-3

Municipal Bond Portfolio Policies: Credit Quality Requirements
(Respondent Banks; by Size Groups)

	Amount of Assets (in Millions of Dollars)		
	To 300	300–1,000	Over 1,000
Minimum Rating Accepted:			
Baa	7	6	5
A	3	7	4
Aa	3	—	—
Nonrated Acceptable:			
Yes	3	2	5
No	10	11	4
Revenues Acceptable:			
Yes	11	13	9
No	2	—	—
Higher Ratings on Revenues Required:			
Yes	7	7	1
No	4	6	8
Independent Credit Evaluations Made:			
Yes	6	9	8
No	7	4	1

of municipals and consequent quality constraints imposed. Although a majority (66 percent) reported that independent credit evaluations were required, heavy reliance on the rating services appeared evident, as only 28 percent would consider nonrated bonds. [8]

Significant policy differences between large and smaller banks are also evident; only a few of the banks in the two smaller size groups would accept nonrated obligations, whereas a majority of the largest group would do so. This difference in policy is explained by the fact that, for the most part, only large banks are staffed with research analysts to conduct independent credit evaluations.

There was a definite split in policy as to the minimum credit quality requirements. About half would accept Baa, most of the others required an A quality rating (high-medium grade), and a few in the smallest size group required Aa quality (high grade). In general, however, no material differences between size groups were evident on this score. This finding is surprising, because intuitively one might expect that the more sophisticated banks would be more inclined to screen the medium-quality universe for acceptable bonds.

Unless a bank has a competent municipal research capability, developments over the past several years would seem to justify a policy of upgrading quality requirements. The de facto default of New York City obligations, which only a short time before had carried an A rating, has been of particular significance in two respects. First, the rating services have become more inclined to revise ratings frequently, especially downward, and the consequence is that there now appears to be an increased exposure of existing Baa obligations to downrating to Ba (a market value classification). Second, it emphasized the point that municipal units can experience serious credit problems and that insistence on adequate credit quality may therefore be prudent.

In view of these developments, a policy to require at least an A rating (or equivalent on nonrated bonds) would seem appropriate for most banks. Evidence that certain Baa obligations are strong credits (not properly rated) may be sufficient reason for allowing exceptions to general policy. Banks are more or less obliged to take reasonable risks on customer loans, but the same obligation does not exist with respect to the acquisition of securities in the secondary markets.

Moreover, as shown in Table 6-4, medium-quality obligations (Baa) provide only a moderate pickup in yield in most years as compared to good-

---

8. A probable major reason for requiring a rating is that under existing regulatory practice, rated bonds of the top four grades (Aaa to Baa) can be carried at amortized cost automatically, whereas lower grades must be carried at market value. In the case of nonrated bonds, examiners require credit justification that the bonds are "equivalent" to at least a Baa obligation.

TABLE 6-4

Municipal Bond Yields by Maturity and Credit Rating: 1970–78

	Average Yield for Year: Percentage								
	1970	1971	1972	1973	1974	1975	1976	1977	1978
2-Year Maturity									
Prime	4.50	3.10	3.00	4.05	4.80	4.21	3.61	3.21	4.35
Good Quality	4.65	3.25	3.10	4.15	4.90	4.37	3.78	3.35	4.45
Medium Quality	5.00	3.45	3.30	4.30	5.10	4.80	4.12	3.66	4.68
Spread: Medium to Good									
(basis pts.)	35	20	20	15	20	43	34	31	23
5-Year Maturity									
Prime	4.85	3.65	3.60	4.25	4.90	4.83	4.23	3.88	4.65
Good Quality	5.00	3.75	3.70	4.35	5.05	4.98	4.41	4.00	4.75
Medium Quality	5.40	4.05	3.95	4.50	5.25	5.48	4.80	4.17	4.93
Spread: Medium to Good									
(basis pts.)	40	30	25	25	20	50	39	17	18
10-Year Maturity									
Prime	5.35	4.35	4.15	4.45	5.15	5.44	4.84	4.35	4.93
Good Quality	5.55	4.45	4.25	4.55	5.25	5.59	5.04	4.47	5.04
Medium Quality	6.00	4.70	4.50	4.70	5.55	6.02	5.38	4.74	5.27
Spread: Medium to Good									
(basis pts.)	45	25	25	15	30	43	34	27	23
20-Year Maturity									
Prime	6.10	5.25	4.95	5.00	5.70	6.29	5.82	5.16	5.50
Good Quality	6.30	5.40	5.05	5.10	5.80	6.42	5.97	5.28	5.62
Medium Quality	6.65	5.70	5.25	5.25	6.20	6.91	6.31	5.45	5.92
Spread: Medium to Good									
(basis pts.)	35	30	20	15	40	49	34	17	30

Source: Salomon Brothers, *An Analytical Record of Yields and Spreads,* Part III, Table 1.

quality bonds (A to Aa). Although yield spreads tend to widen in recession years such as 1970 and 1975, when risk sensitivity on the part of investors (including banks) becomes acute, in general the yield improvement made possible by moving from good-quality obligations to the medium-quality universe has only amounted to about 20 to 30 basis points. Because credit uncertainties associated with medium-quality obligations increase as maturities are extended (the ability to pay within the next year or so may be evaluated more readily than the ability to pay over a ten-year time horizon), the fact that yield spreads have been roughly equivalent over the maturity distribution shown in Table 6-4 would seem to make long-term medium-quality municipals a particularly unattractive sector. The reasonable expectations of increased spreads between medium- and high-quality bonds as maturities are extended has not been fulfilled in the municipal market in most years.

Municipal revenue bonds have become an increasingly important subset of total municipal offerings in accordance with the theory that user charges rather than general taxes should finance many governmental services. Because the quality of revenue sources may vary widely, and because several partial or full defaults have occurred on some large revenue issues (turnpike revenues in particular), it was our hypothesis that many banks might have a negative policy with respect to these obligations. However, our empirical data show that, except for only two banks in the smallest size group, policies toward revenue obligations were positive.[9] However, given the analytical problems involved in evaluating credit risk, a majority of banks with assets of less than $1 billion had a policy of requiring higher ratings on revenues than on general obligations. On the other hand, large banks with in-house capacities for appraising credit did not consider it necessary to upgrade their minimum rating requirements for revenue obligations.

Portfolio configuration: diversification

In the loan portfolio, legal lending limits represent an automatic diversification requirement, but such limits do not apply to general obligations of municipal units. Management must therefore establish appropriate diversification policies. These would logically include: (1) establishing a maximum amount or, alternatively, the portfolio percentage that may be committed to a given credit; (2) establishing a minimum amount for each commitment consistent with the size of the bank so as to avoid portfolio "clutter" (defined as an excessive number of small commitments); and (3) requiring geographic diversification on the grounds that potential credit problems may be regionally distributed. For example, limiting exposure in a given state or region may seem prudent on the basis of a political and economic appraisal of the state or region.

Table 6-5 shows that banks generally impose specific diversification constraints along these lines, although a few indicated a completely ad hoc policy where complete discretion for the structure of the portfolio is given to the investment officer or committee responsible for its management. The only area of significant disagreement evident in the responses was whether

9. My personal view on revenues has been stated as follows: "The adequacy and reliability of the revenue source must be carefully appraised on these bonds, but in general a reasonably sophisticated investor might be attracted to revenue bonds because their mixed reputation has caused them to sell at attractive yields relative to general obligations." D. A. Hayes and W. S. Bauman, *Investments: Analysis and Management*, 3d ed. (New York: Macmillan, 1976), p. 269.

TABLE 6-5

Municipal Bond Portfolio: Diversification Policies
(Respondent Banks; by Size Groups)

	Amount of Assets (in Millions of Dollars)					
	To 300		300–1,000		Over 1,000	
	Yes	No	Yes	No	Yes	No
Policy Requirements:						
Credit limits imposed (maximum)	12	1	10	3	8	1
Limits vary by credit quality	6	7	6	7	7	2
Geographic diversification required	12	1	8	5	7	2
Minimum commitment specified	12	1	11	2	6	3

policies should specifically include a provision that maximum limits be scaled to credit quality rankings. By a heavy majority, the largest banks favored the reduction of maximum limits for medium-quality names, but in the case of the smaller banks the opinion was divided, with a slight majority indicating no scaling of limits. However, a comparison of the data in Table 6-3 with those in Table 6-5 shows that the number of banks requiring A ratings or higher was about the same as the number indicating no need to scale credit limits. If the portfolio is entirely restricted to high-quality names, then of course the need for scaling maximum limits according to credit quality becomes redundant.

Portfolio configuration: maturities

The preferences of respondents with regard to normative maturity structures are shown in Table 6-6. It is important to emphasize that these are normative in nature, because in most cases maturity policies are subject to ad hoc modifications based on interest rate forecasts and desired targets for interest-sensitivity positions. Maturity policies on municipals differed from those on governments in two major respects. First, the front-end-loaded structure dominated governments; and, while a significant number of banks also indicated a preference for this structure in the municipal account, the laddered maturity structure was the most frequent preference. Second, maximum maturity limits are considerably longer on municipals than on governments; only 17 percent indicated a maturity limit of ten years on municipals and a surprising 40 percent allowed maturities of twenty years or more. In contrast, the government portfolio was typically

TABLE 6-6

Municipal Portfolio: Maturity Policies
(Respondent Banks; by Size Groups)

	Amount of Assets (in Millions of Dollars)			% of Total
	To 300	300–1,000	Over 1,000	
Maturity Structure:				
Laddered	7	4	3	40
Front-end loaded	4	6	2	34
Barbell	—	1	2	9
Back-end loaded	—	1	—	3
Ad hoc (no policy)	2	1	2	14
				100%
Maximum Maturity:				
5 years	—	—	—	—
10 years	4	1	1	17
15 years	5	7	3	43
20 years	3	3	2	23
over 20 years	1	2	3	17
				100%

restricted to maturities of ten years or less. These differences suggest that banks generally regard the municipal portfolio as a quasi-permanent account that will provide a higher average yield level on an after-tax basis than any viable alternative in the financial markets. The historical data show municipal yields on intermediate and long bonds have averaged 60 to 65 percent of taxable obligation yields with equivalent ratings; therefore, assuming a marginal tax rate of about 45 percent, municipals have generally been an attractive vehicle for maximizing after-tax net yield spreads.[10]

Because the barbell structure has received much attention in the literature in recent years, its relative lack of popularity among respondents seemed surprising. Even the presumably more sophisticated large banks had not adopted the barbell concept in any significant numbers. As noted in Chapter 5, the barbell structure is designed to encourage active trading management; the fact that it is seldom used in practice suggests that municipal portfolio policies are generally oriented toward obtaining appropriate long-term income returns rather than as a source of trading profits.[11]

10. The yield spread between municipals and taxables has varied through time. For example, in the second quarter of 1979 municipal yields declined to less than 60 percent of taxables. At such junctures only selective purchases of municipals become desirable as the taxable equivalent yield advantage at such relative yield levels becomes negligible.

11. A simulation for the years 1966–72 (inclusive) of the risk/return results on barbell structures compared to laddered structures wherein active management was precluded

If constantly maintained, a static amount in a laddered maturity structure results in de facto dollar averaging of interest rates prevailing through
time on the largest maturity. Suppose, for example, that a $10 million port-
folio has equal $1 million maturities over one through ten years; the ladder
is maintained by investing each year's maturing one-year obligation in ten-
year obligations at prevailing interest rates. Assuming an upsloping yield
curve which, as shown in Table 6–4, has been typical in the municipal
market even during periods of high interest rates (when the government
yield curve becomes inverted), then the laddered structure results in a
sequence of investments in the high sector of the yield curve in each year.
But the portfolio overall has an average maturity of roughly half the long
maturity where each investment takes place. Passive maturity management
is usually associated with the laddered structure; as will be discussed further, however, most banks consider unbalancing the structure on occasion
via ad hoc decisions regarding the employment of funds generated through
maturities or sale programs.

In addition, the typical dynamics of bank fund flows have also compli-
cated the purely passive maturity management policy (laddered structure).
The size of municipal portfolios has not been static, but as shown in the
banking system data in Chapter 2, funds available for municipals have
increased considerably through time, with growth typically concentrated
during periods of low interest rates. Passive management would require
distribution of the new funds over the ladder sequence in roughly equal
amounts. However, this policy would result in less than average returns
because acquisitions would be greatest during low interest rate periods. As
a consequence, some degree of active maturity management is almost
forced on banks. Perhaps the least aggressive option would be to emphasize
short-term bonds with new funds when interest rates are low and then gradually restore the ladder as interest rates move upward. The sharply upsloping yield curve characteristic of low interest rate periods means that opportunity costs of this policy may be temporarily high, and pressure to
maintain adequate net interest spreads via maturity extensions may be
considerable. But these deterrents to optimal maturity management must
be resisted; otherwise, the return on the municipal portfolio may well be
below the average rates prevailing in the municipal market over a period of
years.

The argument for the front-end-loaded structure is based on the following conclusions: (1) the secular trend of interest rates will probably continue to be upward; (2) even the municipal account should provide some

showed less variation per unit of return (higher efficiency) for ladders than for barbells.
Thus only if the market was believed inefficient and trading profits were consequently
available would the barbell be superior. S. P. Bradley and D. B. Crane, "Simulation of
Bond Portfolio Strategies," *Journal of Bank Research,* Summer 1975, pp. 129–34.

degree of liquidity and interest sensitivity, particularly if significant amounts are committed to fixed-rate retail loan programs; and (3) the long-term outlook for the continuation of Reg Q limits on time and savings deposits is doubtful, which means that interest sensitivity of the liability structure may significantly increase over a time frame of five to ten years. A front-end-loaded structure designed to include some moderate flexibility in maturity management might be as follows:

Maturity	Percentage Objective
0 to 5 years	40–70%
5 to 10 years	20–30%
11 to 15 years	10–30%

During high interest rate periods, the account might be distributed 40–30–30 in each maturity category; at such times maturity extension to the policy limits would be desirable.[12] At the other extreme, commitments of new funds and sales of longs might well result in a 70–20–10 distribution during low rate periods. On the whole, given the typical behavior of fund flows and the other considerations mentioned above, a policy of this type would seem a desirable compromise between highly active maturity management (bar-bell) and passive management (laddered).

Municipal Portfolio: Trading Policies

For purposes of indicating degrees of departure from a purely passive "buy and hold" strategy within a given maturity structure, trading policies were defined broadly to include any discretionary management action which alters the composition of the portfolio in order to improve return performance. There are perhaps three major sources of possible improved returns: (1) management of the maturity structure based on the interest rate outlook, (2) concurrent sales and purchases of individual portfolio items based on comparative yields in the market, and (3) sales and repurchases based on tax considerations.[13]

Table 6-7 shows respondents' policies with respect to various aspects of these trading options. As suggested in the preceding section, the minimal

---

12. The assumption is that interest-sensitivity objectives arising from an evaluation of the entire asset and liability system do not constrain the tactical maturity management program. Also, local municipals purchased to accommodate customer needs probably should be excluded from the maturity policy matrix, as these maturity distributions are not entirely under discretionary control of management.

13. These sources are based roughly on the alternative types of bond swaps identified in S. Homer and M. L. Leibowitz, *Inside the Yield Book* (New York: Prentice-Hall and New York Institute of Finance, 1972), Ch. 6.

TABLE 6-7

Municipal Trading Policies
(Respondent Banks; by Size Groups)

	Amount of Assets (in Millions of Dollars)					
	To 300		300–1,000		Over 1,000	
Type of Trading	Yes	No	Yes	No	Yes	No
Maturity Trading*						
Through rollovers at maturity	12	1	10	3	9	—
Through sales and repurchase	8	5	9	4	9	—
Intramarket Trading on Yield Spread Differences†	8	5	6	7	9	—
Intermarket Trading on Yield Spread Differences‡	9	4	8	5	7	2
Tax Loss Trading	8	5	8	5	9	—

*Defined as reducing or extending maturities based on cyclical interest rate outlook.
†Defined as sale and repurchase based on yield spreads between municipal obligations of similar maturity.
‡Defined as shifts between taxables (governments) and municipals based on changes in yield spread relationships between these markets.

degree of active management is to vary the maturity structure as obligations mature or new money becomes available for the portfolio. With only a few exceptions, fund management policies permitted reasonable discretion to invest funds from incremental fund flows or maturing securities into the short or long sections as considered appropriate on the basis of the interest rate outlook. A lesser proportion, but still a majority, had more active maturity management policies which involved the sale of long maturities when the perceived outlook was for higher rates and the converse when the outlook was for falling rates.

Interest rates have been highly volatile over the past decade. As a consequence, profits from maturity swaps would have been considerable if the swaps had been executed correctly. But the risks have also been high for two reasons. First, forecasting models have been notoriously unreliable due largely to the fact that the historical parameters of interest rate fluctuations have had low predictive powers. Second, there is the following observation:

> Maturity swaps are highly speculative. There is often a large penalty if yields do not rise or fall as expected in a short period of time. This is especially true because maturity swaps often involve an immediate loss in yield. This is due to the cyclical behavior of the yield curve which is usually positive....When the swap involves a loss in yield, time works heavily against the swapper. A prompt realignment of yields in the expected direction is often essential for the swap to work

out profitably. If this occurs, the realized gains are usually very large. . . . If extended time periods are involved, coupon income and interest-on-interest will also be important, all of which add up to the realized compound yield.[14]

Therefore, although profits from highly aggressive maturity management policies hypothetically can be large, in general only a moderate degree of activism in this respect seems appropriate for most banks. Moreover, as indicated above, the involuntary increase in liability interest sensitivity during high interest rate periods as Reg Q deposits are disintermediated and replaced with money market certificates or wholesale CDs may also constrain maturity trading (extension of maturities), because the result would be to further reduce both net amounts and the ratio of interest-sensitive assets to liabilities.[15]

Intramarket and intermarket trading is based on the proposition that the bond market is somewhat inefficient, in the sense that differences in market yields may not be justified by differences in the evaluated risk properties of alternative obligations. The reasons for the presumed inefficiencies are complex and controversial, but two receive frequent mention: (1) bond ratings heavily influence market yields and an independent credit analysis may conclude that differences in ratings are not appropriate — that is, an A-rated bond may be evaluated as deserving a higher or lower rating; and (2) large new issues may offer yields above their equivalences in the secondary market. Large banks, with in-house research capabilities for evaluating relative credit quality properties and sophisticated computer and communication facilities to monitor yield relationships in the markets, were strongly inclined to engage in active trading along these lines. Among smaller banks, however, opinion was sharply divided as to the efficacy of such trading policies. Given their limited technical capacities, it is doubtful if many of these banks can achieve significant return improvement through yield pickup swaps, although it probably does no harm to engage in these transactions on an occasional basis, particularly when they involve new issues in the regional area.[16]

---

14. Ibid., pp. 92–93.

15. Several banks reported to the author in the first half of 1979 that this problem was a major factor which inhibited their lengthening of the maturity structure of the municipal portfolio despite their conclusion that interest rates were then at high levels and probably would fall by the end of the year. In view of subsequent events, this was a fortunate constraint because interest rates on municipals advanced considerably, especially in October of that year. The hazards of forecasting were again made clear.

16. A second view is that a significant portion of the municipal portfolio may lack adequate marketability properties and, as a consequence, trading opportunities may be limited. For example, the following observations of a portfolio manager: "It is only among the larger issuers and public housing authority bonds that a reasonable degree of marketability can be assured, and even here large blocs are more difficult to move. In most cases the portfolio manager commits indefinitely to a long-term holding when he acquires

The general applicability of tax loss trading, however, is quite different. Under a special tax provision, banks are allowed to deduct realized capital losses in full from taxable income. Therefore, portfolio returns can be significantly improved by taking such losses during high interest rate periods and reinvesting the proceeds, including the tax savings, into alternative obligations. The format of this evaluation process was illustrated in Table 5–10 and need not be repeated. However, a minor technical addendum might be offered. In the case of municipals, coupon income is completely tax-exempt whereas discount return is taxable at the full corporate rate when realized (either at maturity or at time of sale). Therefore, in the case of municipals, the maximum after-tax yield improvement can usually be achieved by sale of low coupon bonds and their replacement with high coupon bonds or, in other words, replacing discount return with tax-exempt coupon return.

Given the unquestioned advantages of tax loss trading, it seemed surprising to find that ten out of thirty-six respondents, all in the smaller size categories, had not engaged in these transactions. When asked to indicate their reasons for a negative policy toward tax loss management, these banks mentioned the following:[17]

Directors' aversion to loss recognition	3
Lack of tax liability to absorb loss	1
Desire not to reduce reported earnings	8
Lack of marketability of municipals	1

Some of these reasons appear legitimate (lack of tax liability and restricted marketability of holdings), but a general aversion to losses on the part of directors can unequivocally be described as an inefficient policy.

Avoiding realized security losses because of their negative impact on reported earnings may or may not be a legitimate reason. On the one hand, if the losses would result in a significant earnings instability and perhaps trigger shareholder concern, the decision might be justified. On the other hand, banks should recognize that a stable growth trend in earnings is a desirable performance feature. If reported earnings in a given year are likely to increase at a rate well above average, then the use of discretionary realized losses to bring earnings closer to the trend line and to build in a source of earnings growth by means of yield improvement on the portfolio would seem highly desirable.

---

longer-dated tax-exempts." L. S. Prussia, Jr. (Senior Vice-President, Bank of America), in Prochnow and Prochnow (eds.), *The Changing World of Banking* (New York: Harper and Row, 1974), p. 181.

17. Some banks indicated more than one reason for the negative policy on tax management; all reasons given are listed.

7

ORGANIZATION STRUCTURE: POLICY FORMULATION AND IMPLEMENTATION

Funds management usually involves two and sometimes three levels of decision making. At the top level, policy guidelines are established for asset and liability programs, results are monitored, and policy revisions are made as appropriate in light of dynamic changes in local banking markets, regulatory constraints, and the financial markets in general. At the second level, operational decisions are made as required to implement policies within the specific asset and liability sectors. The possible third level would be that of corporate planning involving policy strategies for the acquisition of capital funds to support growth in the asset and liability programs and, possibly, to finance acquisitions or the formation of de novo subsidiaries.

Our concern, however, is with the first two levels only, and even here we are excluding the loan programs. The operative assumption is that discretionary funds management policies are structured primarily to accommodate the needs of established loan programs. As discussed in my study of lending policies,[1] this is not strictly accurate, particularly over a long-term time horizon; however, if it is presumed that banks desire to maintain a strong competitive posture in their major loan markets, then the effective maneuvering room for controlling fund allocations to these markets is quite limited.

Line functions

The preceding chapters have discussed in some detail policy issues with respect to the major asset and liability sectors that are under the effective control of the funds management division of a bank. The operational line functions controlled by these policies may be summarized as follows:

1. Douglas A. Hayes, *Bank Lending Policies: Domestic and International,* 2d ed. (Ann Arbor: University of Michigan, Division of Research, Graduate School of Business Administration, 1977), pp. 224–34.

All banks:
1. Management of liquidity requirements through the acquisition and disposition of money market assets and purchased funds.
2. Management of spread banking operations either on an aggressive basis through active purchase and layoff of funds or on a defensive basis consequent to accommodating customer needs for CD placements.
3. Management of the government and agency bond portfolios.
4. Management of the municipal bond portfolio.
5. Management of the interest-sensitivity position and exposure through integration and control of operational decisions on all of the above.

Some banks (usually large):
1. Conducting dealer operations in specified sectors of the money market, including Fed Funds, governments and agencies, municipals, and Eurocurrencies.
2. Conducting investment banking activities with respect to eligible types of bond issues, principally municipals.
3. Issuing and managing commercial paper sold in the market by the holding company.

Staff support

Effective implementation of the several line activities requires considerable staff support in the form of appropriate information and analysis systems. In large banks the major portion of this support is usually generated in-house. First, there may be an economic analysis section to forecast future interest rate and fund flow probabilities. Second, and perhaps of prime importance, there must be staff support to develop and implement an information system which isolates and projects the major asset and liability items subject to customer action (primarily core deposits and loans) and the pattern of expected revenues and expenses over appropriate future time frames. Liquidity, tax, and interest-sensitivity management all depend on an adequate information system, although reasonable error margins in the projections must, of course, be anticipated and accommodated by funds management decisions.[2] Finally, some large banks have established operations research departments whose primary responsibility may be support of the above staff functions through the formulation and processing of econo-

2. In a series of articles on the development and implementation of a system method of asset and liability management, it was argued that "the building of an integrated accounting system represents about 70 percent of the job of adopting the system method of asset and liability management." J. V. Baker, "System Method of Asset/Liability Management: What It Is, How It Works," *Banking*, Sept. 1978, p. 114.

metric models. These models may include, for example, an econometric interest rate forecast, simulation models designed to show the consequences of alternative funds management decisions on the net interest margin, and linear programming models designed to show the optimal asset mix.[3] In essence, the operations research (management science) operation may be construed as one means of implementing the staff support required both to establish policies and to make the tactical decisions necessary to execute funds management programs.

Organization Structure

Given the line functions and staff support activities outlined above, a table of organization for a large regional bank might be structured along the lines shown in Figure 7-1. It is probable, of course, that each bank would modify this structure to fit individual personnel capabilities and the perceived relative importance of and relationships between the several line functions. However, in the interest of real world authenticity, Figure 7-1 depicts a moderately simplified version of the organization structure of a large regional bank with a reputation for excellent performance in its fund management programs. In moderate-sized banks, separate departments for various components of the portfolio are probably not warranted. Moreover, except for an information system whose purpose is to generate projected balance sheet and income statement data, staff support may be obtained from external sources.

The two levels of management decision authority are indicated in Figure 7-1. To illustrate more specifically the responsibilities at each level, consider the decisions required to structure and manage a municipal bond portfolio. First, management at decision level 1 would establish the policies for the normative configuration of the maturities and the quality and diversification requirements of the portfolio. Second, this level would also control any significant departures from normative objectives based on an evaluation and determination of short-term system targets (interest-sensitivity levels and exposure). At decision level 2, the municipal department would evaluate credit qualities and other significant properties of individual names and would have the authority to execute day-to-day purchases and/or sales based on both the relative ranking of individual names and the policy guidelines received from decision level 1. But communication between the two levels must be constantly maintained in order to assure a reasonable degree of flexibility. For example, suppose a given municipal

---

3. An excellent book that covers in depth the alternative possible applications of quantitative methods to information systems and forecasts is K. S. Cohen and S. E. Gibson (eds.), *Management Science in Banking* (Boston: Warren, Gorham, and Lamont, 1978).

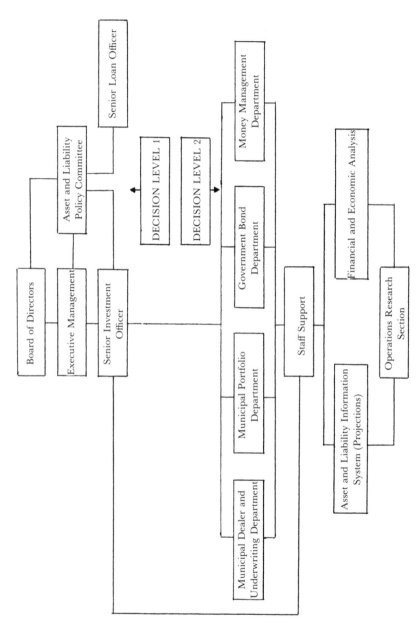

Fig. 7-1. Funds management: table of organization (large banks).

issue, evaluated as attractive on a quality-yield basis, is available in the market, but the purchase of an optimal-sized bloc would result in a departure from some phase of existing policy limits. Immediate communication of the situation to decision level 1, and the existence of some mechanism at that level for prompt ad hoc approval of policy exceptions, would seem highly desirable. Therefore, although for reasons of clarity the following discussion of funds management organization structures isolates the two levels of decision authority, it should be recognized that constant interfaces between levels are highly desirable and that the degree of authority given each level may vary considerably.

Decision level 1

Board of Directors. In the funds management area, the role of the board as a whole is largely that of approving decision level 1 policies and conducting periodic reviews of performance measured against management goals and constraints. The reason for the limited role of directors is that their technical competence to participate actively in policy strategy and tactical implementation is usually very limited. But for several reasons a compelling argument can be made that one or more outside board members should be qualified to participate more actively in these matters. The principal reason is that the personal legal liability of bank directors is clearly greater than is the case for directors of nonfinancial corporations. For example, a review of legal precedents prompted the following observation:

> It follows that, where losses occur, to exculpate the director it is not enough that no actual dishonesty can be shown, or other misbehavior. Neither ignorance nor inexperience may be pleaded as an excuse, for, the FDIC holds, one who voluntarily takes the position of director undertakes that he possesses at least ordinary knowledge and skill and that he will bring them to bear in the discharge of his duties.[4]

Given the legal ambiguities as to the extent of their personal liability, it would seem prudent for the board to include at least one member qualified to monitor, evaluate, and perhaps participate in the funds management operations at decision level 1. These individuals may also make valuable contributions to policy dynamics, particularly in moderate-sized banks where financial market expertise may be limited. Finally, the explicit requirement that policies and implementation strategies be articulated and rationalized to an outside director with technical competence in the area may well provide motivation to conduct more careful study of the issues and options than would otherwise be the case.

Asset and Liability Management Committee. In many banks, the primary

---

4. American Bankers Association, *A Bank Director's Job,* 13th ed. (Washington, D.C.: ABA, 1970), p. 3.

responsibility for establishment of decision level 1 policies has been assigned to a formal asset and liability management committee (ALCO). As of the end of 1978, about 70 percent (twenty-five out of a universe of thirty-six) of the respondents had a formal ALCO which met at least once a month.[5] Our original hypothesis was that this committee would be concerned primarily with specific investment portfolio strategies and might possibly become involved in individual portfolio decisions. Indeed, as shown in Table 7-1, investment strategy functions dominate its activities, and in several banks its authority was extended to include the initiation of specific transactions and the establishment of rate limits on purchased funds.

However, a number of respondents indicated that the hypothesized functions did not capture all the major policy deliberations of this group, and the addendum to Table 1 gives the views of a number of individual banks with respect to the functions of the ALCO. Although the ALCO may prescribe targets for the amounts, yields, and maturities of the several investment portfolios, these comments suggest that in a number of banks ALCO deliberations and decisions concentrate more on systems management strategy—that is, establishing appropriate interest-sensitivity positions (exposures) and spread management yield targets—than on individual portfolio policies. In brief, the asset and liability management committee seems increasingly to be charged with setting policy targets and guidelines for system objectives, in addition to establishing operational policies for liquidity management and for the several sectors of the investment portfolio.

Given these broad system responsibilities, the composition of the committee would at a minimum include the CEO, the senior investment officer, one or more senior loan officers to provide information as to loan demand, and a staff officer to provide current data on the asset and liability system and projections thereof. In addition, it is notable that several banks included outside directors on the committee and that all operational policies and decisions had to be formally approved by the entire board of directors each month.

Senior Investment Officer. As shown in Figure 7-1, the responsibility for transmitting ALCO policy guidelines to the several departments and monitoring their implementation usually devolves upon one individual. Indeed, in moderate-sized banks the investment officer may also implement policies across the board because the size of the portfolio does not justify separate departmental breakdowns. In fact, because the major investment portfolio

---

5. In those banks where a formal committee was not used, the CEO and/or the investment officer were responsible for policy determination. As might be expected, this was more typical in small banks than in large banks.

items (governments, municipals, and money market instruments) are acquired on an impersonal basis in units of relatively large size, a single individual with moderate staff support can effectively manage (assuming ALCO policy direction) a large portfolio of perhaps $100 million or more.

TABLE 7-1

Functions of Asset and Liability Committees
(Respondent Banks; by Size Groups)

| Function | Amount of Assets (in Millions of Dollars) | | | | | |
| | To 300 | | 300-1,000 | | Over 1,000 | |
	Yes	No	Yes	No	Yes	No
Establish targets (yields) on portfolio acquisitions	9	—	8	—	6	2
Establish targets (prices) on portfolio sales	8	1	7	1	7	1
Authorize specific portfolio transactions	3	6	3	5	1	7
Approve CD rates on purchased funds	2	7	2	6	2	6
Review and change maturity targets on portfolios	8	1	7	1	5	3

Addendum (Other functions as listed by banks):

- Review and analyze variances to profit plan and develop strategies for maximizing "balance sheet" income
- Approval of policy and strategy as recommended by investment officer on a quarterly basis
- Committee sets policies and targets for all asset groups as well as portfolio
- Review credit quality of investment securities; decide degree of usage of purchased funds; determine minimum acceptable interest rate spreads in relation to interest arbitrage operations; determine amount of securities gains or losses to be realized for tax purposes and financial reporting purposes. Determine optimal overall portfolio size and composition
- Review all trading account policies, money market source and use limits, and international lending activity limits
- Policy committee which manages rate sensitivity gap and establishes broad guidelines governing asset-liability trends
- Committee also sets loan rates and decides marketing emphasis to accomplish goals

This is in marked contrast to the loan sectors where lack of homogeneity of loan types and the need to structure commercial loans to the specific financing requirements of customers necessarily results in a more extensive departmental structure even in banks of moderate size.

In large banks, however, the senior investment officer may find it desirable to operate through a formal departmental structure along the lines outlined in Figure 7–1, for two reasons. First, because large amounts, perhaps a billion dollars or more, may be committed to each portfolio area, the use of a number of specialists in research analysis and trading techniques may be efficient, even if their contributions add only a few basis points to total returns on average. Second, certain funds management operations and peripheral activities require full-time specialist personnel to conduct them effectively, and these activities are mostly unique to large banks. They include: (1) dealer operations in money market instruments (Feds Funds), (2) interest arbitrage activities on a continuous basis, (3) use of global funding sources on a large scale wherein small cost differences between a host of alternative instruments become significant, and (4) underwriting of municipal bond issues and conducting of dealer operations in selected municipals and governments. Given these complexities, the senior investment officer becomes largely an administrative officer and only occasionally may be involved in the execution of specific transactions.

Decision level 2

Money Management Department. This department is essentially charged with managing the purchased funds position of a bank; usually this includes the dealer operation in money market instruments.[6] As noted elsewhere, consistent net dealer positions in Fed Funds purchased may represent a significant source not only of dealer spread returns but also of quasi-permanent funds. Because purchased funds have become the normative source for handling short-term and seasonal liquidity requirements, this department essentially manages these two dimensions of liquidity.

In addition, responsibility for conducting interest arbitrage operations would logically be assigned to this department. Therefore, while the primary concern of this group is the acquisition of purchased funds in various forms and from various sources, responsibility for acquisition of a limited universe of short-term asset instruments (such as commercial paper, bankers' acceptances, and perhaps Eurodollar placements) might also be assigned to this department. Management of the "due from banks" account, which includes the reserve account at the Fed, CDs of other

---

6. Eurocurrency dealer operations and funding of the international loan position may be included, although this may be delegated to an offshore branch (London, usually) if the branch is large and staffed with specialists in these areas.

banks, and correspondent accounts, would also logically be their responsibility. Because very large amounts may be involved even in regional banks (with assets up to $1 billion or more), rigorous decision level 1 policy constraints may be imposed including (1) maturity gap limits, (2) dealer position limits, and (3) amount and maturity limits on wholesale CDs and short-term borrowings.

Government Bond Department. Given the declining role of governments and agencies in bank portfolios, plus the fact that roughly the same technical expertise — trading skills and sensitivity to market conditions — is required here as in the money management department, a logical policy issue is whether a separate department is required to manage this sector. Although the answers to this inquiry were not completely convincing, the major argument is that the money management department is largely concerned with short-term market conditions, such as the probable level of Fed Funds rates over the next several days or weeks, whereas the government bond department focuses largely on the cyclical outlook for interest rates and manages the portfolio so as to maintain a maturity configuration appropriate to this outlook. In addition, this department may engage in technical bond swaps, often involving new issue subscriptions and sale of similar maturity obligations at modest yield pickups. Finally, some large banks are major government bond dealers and as such maintain dealer positions which are reflected on the position statement in a separately reported trading account. Presumably, the government bond department would also have responsibility for this operation.

Municipal Bond Department. In contrast to governments, the role of municipals in bank portfolios has increased significantly over the last decade or so. Moreover, recent credit problems of a few municipal units — New York and Cleveland may be cited as examples — have shown that bond ratings should not be the sole grounds for credit assessments and that in-depth research should be conducted into the credit qualities of municipal obligations considered for the portfolio. Not surprisingly, demand for municipal analysts has enjoyed a growth track in recent years in marked contrast to most areas of security analysis. In fact, inability to find sufficient numbers of competent municipal bond analysts was cited by some banks as a problem.

Within the department, the organization may include specialists, such as one or more analysts assigned to handle revenue bonds or to cover a given geographic region with identifiable demographic and economic trends. The department may have authority to buy and sell individual issues within broad policy limits established at decision level 1. Alternatively, limits on authority may be prescribed, with purchases (sales) above a certain amount requiring the approval of the investment officer.

In our model bank complete responsibility for execution of purchases and sales (trading) was lodged within the department. The following may be argued in support of this arrangement: (1) municipal markets are fragmented except on a relatively few national names and (2) a large proportion of purchases may be acquired through new issue subscriptions rather than in the secondary market because bloc size is often inadequate in the latter market. Similarly, the sale of large blocs may require effort almost commensurate with a secondary distribution.[7] Therefore, normal secondary market trading techniques apply only partially to the municipal market, although the distinction is less important for smaller banks that buy and sell in blocs of $100,000 or less.

As shown in Figure 7-1, large banks may have a separate municipal dealer and underwriting department. This activity is purely investment banking, and probably should be completely divorced from the funds management process in order to avoid possible conflicts of interest. Unusually high long or short positions arising from mistakes in dealer or underwriting commitments should not be remedied by sale to or acquisitions from the bank portfolio. Therefore, the municipal bond department should conduct transactions with the dealer and underwriting department only if it can be clearly documented that outside dealers offer less favorable terms.

Staff support

As shown in Figure 7-1, staff support may be useful at both decision levels. However, the staff concerned with developing and maintaining effective asset and liability information systems would function primarily to support the higher level of policy decisions; ALCO committee deliberations especially require an effective system analysis.

It is necessary, of course, to have a mechanical information system to support management of the legal reserve position (holding no excess reserves at all times) and to compute the maturity gap on interest arbitrage operations. But because these data systems are required for daily (or even hourly) tactical decisions, they are properly lodged within the line department assigned these responsibilities.

Financial and economic analysis

Large banks typically employ one or more financial economists in senior staff positions whose duties usually include activities well beyond assistance to the funds management process. For example, their responsibilities might include responses to regulatory proposals, preparation of position papers

---

7. For this reason some banks have the normative policy of holding municipals until maturity and consider sales only for special reasons such as tax management considerations. In brief, cyclical adjustment of the maturity configuration may involve excessive opportunity costs relative to prospective returns. For the same reason, bond swap operations are of limited feasibility in this area.

on political and economic issues for the media, and analyses of demographic trends within the market area. In the case of small banks, economic consultants may be retained to provide economic and financial market analyses on a regular or "as required" basis. But whether prepared in-house, purchased from outside consultants, or obtained in some other way, some means of appraising the cyclical and long-term outlook for the financial markets (interest rates) is required in order to structure and implement funds management policies. In addition, although the initiative for estimating prospective loan demand might rest with the various loan departments, an independent staff review of these estimates in light of probable local and national economic conditions might be very useful.

Although the value of staff inputs along the above lines might seem obvious, experience has suggested that great care must be exercised in converting forecast data into funds management decisions. Because the economy and financial markets have been subject to a series of unexpected shocks in recent years, many if not most specific forecasts have been seriously flawed. It might therefore be quite appropriate to take a defensive implementation posture rather than to assume the risks of error associated with aggressive implementation. Indeed, a study of variations in the net interest margins of a set of major banks during 1972–76, a period marked by significant swings in interest rates in both directions, showed widely diverse performances; some banks enjoyed significant rewards from aggressive tactics, but the performance of others was very disappointing.[8] But a defensive implementation means only that the asset and liability system be managed so that radical departures from a balanced position (an interest sensitivity ratio of 1) be constrained—not that a constant balanced position be maintained. Tolerating even moderate variations in the interest-sensitivity exposure requires some implicit or explicit assessment of the probabilities of future interest rates.

Operations research

As shown in Figure 7-1, computerized econometric models developed through the application of operations research methods represent one means of analyzing data to provide the information required by both major staff departments. In an organizational sense, therefore, the operations research section constitutes staff support for staff support. But because econometric model construction and manipulation requires sophisticated competence in mathematical statistics, concentration of these activities in a separate unit has been the typical practice in large banks. In-house capability is not required, however, as a number of models are available for purchase from consulting firms specializing in their construction and inter-

8. D. C. Cates, "Interest Sensitivity in Banking," *Bankers Magazine,* Jan.–Feb. 1978, p. 24.

pretation. Thus, it is possible for even moderate-sized banks to use operations research methods as part of their staff data systems.[9]

Four types of models designed to assist funds management may be identified: (1) comprehensive asset and liability optimization models, (2) economic and interest rate forecasting models, (3) simulation models to show the possible results of alternative asset and liability strategies, and (4) specific application models constructed to assist in the management of a particular sector.[10]

Table 7–2 shows respondent banks' patterns of usage of econometric models in their funds management operations. Large banks without exception indicated that one or more types of models were used in their planning processes. Simulation programs were universal, and most also used interest rate forecasting and customer analysis models. However, opinion was sharply divided with respect to the desirability of asset allocation optimization models, which are usually based on linear programming techniques.

TABLE 7–2

Financial Model Usage
(Respondent Banks; by Size Groups)

	Amount of Assets (in Millions of Dollars)					
	To 300		300–1,000		Over 1,000	
	Yes	No	Yes	No	Yes	No
Usage of Financial Models	6	7	7	6	9	—
Types Used:						
Asset/liability optimization	4	2	3	4	5	4
Forecasting	3	3	3	4	6	3
Simulation	5	1	7	—	9	—
Specific application:						
Legal reserve	2	4	1	5	4	5
Interest sensitivity	1	5	6	1	5	4
Customer analysis	2	4	5	2	7	2

Others Listed by Respondents:
  1. Bond portfolio swapping program
  2. Regression analysis to project major asset and liability categories

9. Most of the respondent banks with less than $1 billion in assets that used models indicated that in-house capabilities were limited so far as sophisticated models were concerned.

10. The potential use of all these various types of models is very well illustrated in Cohen and Gibson, *Management Science in Banking.* It also should be noted that operations research techniques are applicable to areas outside of funds management activities, such as personnel staffing needs, branch locations, and operations.

In the case of smaller banks only half indicated any use of models; but like the large banks, simulation models were the primary type in general use. In addition, moderate-sized banks made considerable use of specific application models, especially in the areas of interest-sensitivity and customer account analysis.[11]

Because asset/liability optimization models are designed to provide major staff support to decision level 1, the controversy surrounding their use should be briefly considered. The objectives of one such model were described as follows:

> The linear programming model helps bank executives determine an optimal sequence of balance sheet positions for the bank over a multi-period planning horizon which stretches several years into the future. This sequence of balance sheets is said to be "optimal" in that it results in the largest possible present value of the bank's net income, subject to a variety of constraints on the bank's safety, liquidity, and other relevant considerations, and given the bank's initial balance sheet position and its economic forecasts over the planning horizon.[12]

This model generated specific targets for the major asset and liability components and was designed so that solutions could be varied in line with alternative forecast probabilities. Certainly as a device to assist management in developing a system rather than a sector approach to funds management policies, a model of this type has much to recommend it. In addition, simulation of the effects of different constraints and forecasts should provide a basis for appraising the potential risk-reward trade-offs of alternative policies, while clearly indicating that continual monitoring and revisions of policies and implementation tactics are required in a dynamic and uncertain world.[13]

But the major problem encountered in their practical use as a guide to funds management policies has been that the range of reasonably estimated forecast parameters required to drive the models has been repeatedly violated in recent years. In reviewing the use of these comprehensive models, a high-level banker indicated the consequences as follows:

> Events of recent years have hastened the disenchantment of management. Forecasts of interest rates and other variables were needed to drive the models. And

---

11. Because algebraic equations may not be involved in these specific application models, they are not derived from operations research techniques as generally understood. However, they represent "models" in that they set up a formalized abstract set of relationships to analyze quantitative data generated from one or more departments within the bank (including forecasts) in a form that may be useful for decision making.

12. K. J. Cohen, "Dynamic Balance Sheet Management: A Management Science Approach," *Journal of Bank Research* 2, no. 4 (Winter 1972), p. 11.

13. The proponents of this approach have never held a single solution to be universally appropriate but have always emphasized the need to make multiple and recurrent runs of the model to incorporate various forecast scenarios. Ibid., pp. 13–14.

when interest rates unexpectedly shot up to record levels, strategies that might have been optimal under more stable circumstances proved to be distinctly less than optimal with widely fluctuating rates.[14]

This comment suggests that relatively stable financial market conditions (or, alternatively, correct estimates of the range of fluctuations) are essential in order for these models to make a significant contribution to funds management decisions. Indeed an empirical study based on the relatively stable conditions of 1971–72 reached the following conclusion:

> Our results suggest that the scope of the predictive problem is large compared to the allocational problem in bank resource applications. In our experiment, the value of the optimizing logic of our programming structure is reduced due to the predictive errors in future interest rates, loan demand, and deposit levels.... Although further development and refining of programming models is likely to lead to further improvement in the allocational efficiency of bank planning structures, our results suggest that the biggest unrealized gain in bank planning efficiency associates with improvements in forecasting accuracy.[15]

Given the fact that the forecasting record, particularly in regard to cyclical movements in interest rates, has been notoriously subject to major "predictive errors," McKinney's conclusions on the use of comprehensive asset/liability optimization models as staff support for funds management decisions would seem entirely valid:

> (1) ...in the area of funds management, at least, it is neither necessary nor desirable for these smaller banks to look to models. Essentially, the problem of funds management is that of weighting the bank's balance sheet so as to optimize over time the competing needs for profit, safety, and liquidity. The small banker cannot spend a great deal of time worrying about an eighth or sixteenth of a point. Generally, he makes a greater contribution to his bank's profits by tending to the quality and volume of his business.
>
> (2) The number of variables is clearly so great, and their susceptibility to random influences so important, that it simply is not practical for a bank to try to put them into any large-scale mathematical model. It would cost too much and the results would not be that much more reliable than what can be attained by much more simplistic approaches....Most large banks have moved away from the large-scale model, but are making quite effective use of the computer and quantitative techniques to support specific decisions. It is hard to give management all the aids it needs at the detailed decision level, but we seem unable to provide large-scale models of any real use other than as a teaching aid.[16]

---

14. G. W. McKinney, "A Perspective on the Use of Models in the Management of Bank Funds," *Journal of Bank Research,* Summer 1977, p. 123.

15. M. E. Echols and J. W. Scott, "Forecasting vs. Allocational Efficiency in Bank Asset Planning," *Journal of Bank Research,* Winter 1976, p. 294.

16. McKinney, pp. 126–27.

Experiments with the application of operations research techniques to provide useful data and information for funds management decisions will and should continue, particularly in large banks that have the in-house resources to support the research. But in the present state of the art, simulation models to evaluate the possible outcomes of alternative policies and specific application models—interest-sensitivity position and exposure analysis, for example—are probably the most appropriate areas for the development and use of quantitative methods.

In the preceding chapters, a number of analytical formats designed to assist in the formulation and implementation of funds management policies have been suggested. But as emphasized by McKinney, bank funds management is principally an art rather than a science, and managerial skills, intelligence, and prudence will continue to be the prime requisites of successful fund management operations in commercial banks.

APPENDIX

The questionnaire reproduced below is a facsimile of the one used in this study to obtain the views of a selected sample of banks on funds management policies and practices.

Management Goals and Processes

1. Has your bank established a set of specific financial goals against which performance can be measured?

2. If answer to (1) is yes, do these goals include:
   a. Return on assets?
   b. Return on equity?
   c. Growth rate in earnings?
   d. Growth rate in core deposits?
   e. Growth rates in purchased funds?
   f. Growth rates in total assets?
   g. Dividend payout ratio?
   h. Other? (please specify briefly)

3. Has your bank established a specific set of constraints as a guide to management policies and/or to facilitate forward planning?

4. If answer to (3) is yes, do these constraints include:
   a. Total capital to assets (or assets less cash)?
   b. Total capital to deposits?
   c. Equity capital to assets?
   d. Loan-deposit ratio?
   e. Risk assets to capital?
   f. Governments to deposits?
   g. Other? (please specify briefly)

5. Does your bank construct and use mathematical models to assist in asset and liability management decisions?

6. If so, do they include the following:
   a. Model of profit maximization based on optimal asset mix subject to prescribed constraints and based on forecasts of exogenous variables?
   b. Models designed to forecast interest rates and other key variables, such as deposit and loan growth?
   c. Simulation models to determine effects of alternative asset and liability decisions on earnings?
   d. Model to supply information for and compute legal reserve requirements?
   e. Interest-sensitivity model to compute and track interest-sensitivity position?
   f. Customer account profitability model to analyze account profitability?
   g. Other? (please specify briefly)

7. Does your bank have a formal asset and liability management committee that meets regularly?

8. If so, do the functions of the committee include:
   a. Establish policies (targets) for instruments to be acquired during intervals between meeting?
   b. Establish policies (targets) for instruments to be sold during intervals between meeting?
   c. Make actual decisions on portfolio sales and purchases?
   d. Approve or decide yields on large CDs?
   e. Review and change maturity targets on:
      1. government portfolio?
      2. municipal portfolio?
   f. Other? (please specify briefly)

9. If a committee is not used to determine portfolio policies, please indicate title of person (persons) responsible for such policies and their implementation.

Liquidity Management

1. Does your bank make specific projections of loan demand and levels of core deposits (demand and retail savings and time)?
   a. How often are projections made:
      Monthly? Quarterly? Semi-annually? Yearly?
   b. Maximum time horizon: _____

2. Does your bank have a seasonal pattern to loan demand and core deposit levels defined as different rates of growth or possible declines at certain periods of each year of these items?

   a. If seasonal liquidity requirements are perceived, does the bank use the following funding sources (please indicate priority of sources under normal circumstances by placing numbers 1, 2, 3, 4 opposite each option):
1. Federal Funds purchased
2. Repos
3. Large CDs ($100,000 or more)
4. Liquidate short-term assets (Fed Funds, T-bills, etc.)

   b. Are any policy limits as to total amounts placed on the following liabilities:
      Fed Funds purchased
      Repos
      Large CDs ($100,000 or more)
      Total short-term borrowings
1. Are limits, if any, in terms of:
      Specified dollar amounts?
      Percentage of assets or deposits?
      Other? (please specify)

3. To cover short-term random fluctuations (daily or weekly) in deposits (and loans), does your bank regularly use:
   a. Fed Funds sold
   b. Fed Funds purchased
   c. Repos
   d. Other (please specify)

4. Under tight money conditions (1974 and possibly 1978), which of the following conditions describe the experience of your bank? Please check those applicable.
1. Decline in Reg Q-limited deposits
2. Loan growth exceeds core deposit growth
3. Reduced margin between core deposit growth and loan growth greater than considered "normal," but core deposit growth still exceeds loan growth
4. No effect apparent on either deposits or loan accounts as compared to other years

   a. Does your bank hold liquid assets as a precautionary secondary reserve to cover a tight money contingency as expressed by (1) and (2) above?

   b. Would the following liabilities be considered appropriate to fund a tight money liquidity strain (loan demand exceeding deposit growth):
1. Short-term borrowing (Fed Funds or Repos)
2. Large CDs issued
      To customers

> To noncustomers
> To investment dealers

c. If any item of (b) is yes, would the emphasis on asset liquidation (money market assets or other portfolio sales) or use of purchased funds depend on one or more of the following considerations? Please check those applicable:

    1. Cost of purchased funds compared to book yield on assets considered for sale

    2. Cost of purchased funds compared to market yield of assets considered for sale

    3. Perceived ability to incur losses on sale of assets

    4. Perceived reliability of purchased fund sources

    5. Policy limits on purchased funds

    6. Need to constrain total risk asset position

    7. Other (please specify)

d. During the 1973–78 period inclusive:

    1. Has your bank always paid maximum Reg Q rates on savings and time deposits?

    2. If not, did you increase rates to maximum allowed under Reg Q in 1974? 1978?

    3. Does your bank currently offer the new $10,000 minimum money market certificates?

    4. If answer to (1), (2), and/or (3) is no, please specify principal reason.

Spread Management

1. Does your bank regularly monitor its "interest-sensitivity" position:

    a. Through ratios of interest-sensitive assets to interest-sensitive liabilities?

    b. Through total amount of interest-sensitive assets to interest-sensitive liabilities?

2. Are "interest-sensitive" assets and liabilities broken down according to maturities of:

    a. 1 month or less

    b. 3 months

    c. 6 months

    d. 1 year

    e. Other (please specify)

3. Does your bank manage the interest-sensitivity position in the sense that positive steps are taken to shorten asset maturities and lengthen liability maturities when it appears that interest rates may move higher

over the next several months or so and vice versa when it appears that rates may decline?

4. Does your bank actively solicit large CDs (over $100,000) or short-term borrowings for direct allocation to investment assets based on a profitable interest spread between cost of funds and return on assets wherein:

	CDs	Borrowings
a. maturities of liabilities and assets are roughly the same?		
b. maturities of acquired assets exceed maturities of acquired liabilities (yield curve upsloping currently)?		
c. maturities of acquired assets less than maturities of acquired liabilities (yield curve down-sloping)?		

5. Has your bank used short-term borrowings (Fed Funds, Repos) to acquire money market assets when a positive yield spread has existed?

6. Has your bank used large CDs or short-term borrowings to acquire Eurodollar CDs?

Governments and Agencies

1. Does your bank have a policy as to the normative size of the government portfolio?

2. Is this determined by (please check applicable items):
   a. Percentage of deposits
   b. Percentage of assets
   c. Other (please specify)

3. Are agencies considered full substitutes for governments?
   a. If yes, would you include pass-through securities like GNMA certificates?
   b. Do you ever buy agency securities for future or delayed delivery (beyond 30 days)?

4. Does the functional role of governments in the portfolio include the following? (Please list by priority of function by indicating 1, 2, 3, 4, 5, 6; if functions are not applicable leave blank.)
   a. Secondary reserves for liquidity needs
   b. Pledging requirements
   c. Limiting risk asset exposure

d. Window dressing (maintain "appropriate" amounts of cash and governments to satisfy bank analysts, depositors, or shareholders)

e. To satisfy regulatory authorities or requirements

f. Return attraction relative to alternatives on risk/reward evaluation

5. Is your maturity distribution of the government portfolio characterized by the following:

    1. roughly equal maturities over a specified range?

    2. larger percentages in short maturities with lesser percentages in larger issues?

    3. barbell portfolios (combination of shorts and longs with little in between)?

    a. Do you have a general policy as to the maximum maturity on the government portfolio? If so, please specify maximum limit in years.

6. Do you change the maturity structure of the government and agency account based on the perceived outlook for interest rates?

7. If so, what is maximum average maturity and maximum absolute maturity that would be allowed when interest rates are high and expected to decline?

    Average _____ years
    Maximum _____ years

8. What is the process of maturity extension?

    a. Gradual as rates move higher

    b. Significant intermittent shifts at set target levels

9. Have liquidity considerations inhibited active management of the government and agency portfolio (in the sense that when interest rates are high, the government portfolio must be constrained to fund other needs) in:

    a. 1969–70

    b. 1974–75

    c. 1978

10. Do you take realized losses in periods of high interest rates in order to improve future yields or extend maturity on your government portfolio?

Municipal Bond Portfolio

1. Quality and Diversification Issues (nonlocal names)

    a. Does your bank make independent evaluations of credit qualities?

    b. In general, what is the lowest quality rating you will accept (please check one):

    Baa

A

Aa

Aaa

c. Will you buy the following nonrated municipals?
    1. Local
    2. Nonlocal
d. Are maximum limits placed on amount of one credit that will be acquired?
e. Do these limits vary according to quality ranking (lower limits on lower quality names)?
f. Do you have a requirement for a *minimum* amount of each purchase (no purchases, say, under 100,000 bloc)?
g. Do you require geographic diversification of the portfolio (i.e., limit on amounts from units in particular states)?
h. Does your policy allow for acquisition of revenue bonds as well as general obligations?
i. If the answer to (h) is yes, do you typically require higher ratings for revenues than general obligations (A general accepted, but Aa quality required on revenue, for example)?

2. Maturity Policies
   a. Which of the following best describes your normative maturity distributions?
      1. Staggered, roughly equal maturities over period of years with maximum maturity specified
      2. Barbell account with short maturities (3 years or less) and long maturities (10 years or more) with none or smaller amounts in maturities of years in between
      3. Declining staggered maturities (larger percentages in 1–5 years, lesser percentage in 6–10 years, and even lower percentage over 10 years, as example)
      4. Maturity distribution on ad hoc basis; buy whatever maturity seems attractive at the time without regard to maturity balancing of portfolio
   b. What is maximum maturity that you will accept in account? (Please check one or specify limit)
      a. 5 years
      b. 10 years
      c. 15 years
      d. 20 years
      e. over 20 years

3. Do you deliberately lengthen or shorten maturities in the light of your perception of the interest rate outlook:
   a. Through rollovers of maturing obligations?

    b. Through sale of existing holdings and reinvestment at a different maturity?

4. Do you monitor yields and yield spreads in the secondary market and sell names with relatively lower yields to reinvest in those with relatively high yields (roughly equal maturities and quality)?

5. Do you have a profit plan and/or balance sheet projection which sets target levels for the municipal portfolio for the following year?
    a. If so, is this target largely a "residual" in the sense that it absorbs deposit growth not required for loans and asset liquidity?
    b. Is the amount of the municipal portfolio constrained in any way by:
        1. Capital adequacy considerations (risk asset levels)
        2. Liquidity considerations
    c. Do your projections include a tax liability plan?

6. Do you shift from taxables (governments) to municipals or vice versa depending on yield spread relationships between the two markets?

7. Do you take realized losses in periods of high interest rates in order to improve future yields on the following portfolios:
        1. Governments
        2. Agencies
        3. Municipals
    a. If answer to (7) is no, is the policy against taking realized losses due to:
        1. Management decision
        2. Directors' decision
        3. Lack of tax liability to charge loss against
        4. Desire not to reduce reported earnings
        5. Other (please specify)

8. Do you actively bid on local municipal issues (defined as those government units that have accounts at your bank)?
    a. Do you invite correspondent banks to participate in such bids? (Please check one of the following)
    Often
    Sometimes
    Rarely
    Never